Chelsea Football Club

The Official History in Pictures

'The Big Game' by P.J. Crook, acrylic on canvas and wood, 34 × 43 inches, private collection.

'It was actually a commission for the bookmaker, Victor Chandler, who was presenting it to someone who was a great Chelsea fan. I've always loved Chelsea as the players are so international and all very beautiful.' P.J. Crook (2006)

Chelsea

Football Club

The Official History in Pictures

Rick Glanvill

headline

For my parents

'Your past is a banner.
Your present is a lesson.'

'They are a cosmopolitan, philosophical tribe down in west London. They march with the times, sometimes ahead of it: they accept change, knowing that nothing remains static.' *Geoffrey Green*

Rick Glanvill wholeheartedly thanks Julian Flanders, David Wilson and Lorraine Jerram at Headline, his literary agent, the delightful Cat Ledger, Martin Burgess, Adam Burrage, Jose Cheshire, Crystal Stream Audio for the Norman Long CD 'A song, a smile and a piano', Jackie Cundall, Lyn Davies, Mike Geen, Paul and Roy Goulden, Ron Gourlay, Hugh Hastings, Roger Hayter, George Hilsdon, Ron Hockings, Richard Humphreys, Gladys Hunt, Andy Jackson, Michael Janes, Dave Johnstone, Colm Kerrigan, Matthew Lewis, Carole McDonald, Roy Mitchell, José Mourinho, Paul Roberts, Gary Staker, Kirsten Stein, Robert Stein, Peter Trenter and Gianfranco Zola. Also the staff at the British Library Colindale and King's Cross, the V&A, Bernice at Fulham Age Concern, Hazel Cook at K&C Local Studies, Adam Walczak for his help with the historic kits and all the interviewees.

First published in 2006
by HEADLINE PUBLISHING GROUP

First published in paperback in 2007
by HEADLINE PUBLISHING GROUP

1

Cataloguing in Publication Data is available from the British Library

ISBN 978 0 7553 1468 3

Edited and designed by Butler and Tanner, Frome, Somerset

Printed and bound in France by Pollina. L42737

Headline's policy is to use papers that are natural, renewable and recyclable products and made from wood grown in sustainable forests. The logging and manufacturing processes are expected to conform to the environmental regulations of the country of origin.

Cover photographs © Empics, Colorsport, Getty Images and Offside, and from the collections of Mike Geen and the Chelsea Football Club Centenary Museum.

HEADLINE PUBLISHING GROUP
A division of Hachette Livre UK Ltd
338 Euston Road
London NW1 3BH

www.headline.co.uk
www.hodderheadline.com

ASSOCIATION RULES.

NEW PROFESSIONAL FOOTBALL CLUB.—It has been decided to form a professional football club, to be called the Chelsea Football Club, for Stamford-bridge. Applications will be made for admission to the first division of the Southern League.

The Times (11 March 1905)

Contents

Foreword by Gianfranco Zola

When I arrived at Chelsea in 1996 I didn't know too much about the club I was joining. Obviously I knew about Ruud Gullit and the big players, but I had no idea what a big love affair I would start with the supporters there and what a great club it is, with a wonderful history.

I stayed for seven years, more than 300 wonderful games and many medals, and the fans were always there for me, through the good and the not so good times. In Italy they think of English fans as being cool. This is wrong I think. Although the pressure on a footballer is not so great in England because the public is so polite, they are still very, very passionate football people. I rediscovered the simple joy of football at Chelsea.

On the club staff too there were always many people with Chelsea in their heart, telling me all the time about a fantastic game from the past, or a brilliant player – 'Hey Franco, you would have loved playing alongside Kerry Dixon, Peter Osgood.'

I was also lucky enough to meet some of the men that are true legends, especially during the centenary events. I always liked talking with Ossie, Charlie Cooke, Frank Blunstone, Roy Bentley, Pat Nevin and many, many more. All of us Blue.

You can't imagine what it meant to be voted Chelsea's 'greatest ever player' in 2003. Incredible. Thank you again. A real honour that still makes me very humble, and it was presented to me by my dear friend, and another Chelsea 'legend': Lord Attenborough.

Now I am only in the history of Chelsea, not the present. When I left it was really touching so many people wrote to me with good wishes, and even came to support me in Sardinia! That was incredible. It makes me proud when I still hear my name sung at matches even now. I saw the fans' emotional tributes to Peter Osgood when he died and I was not at all surprised. It just shows again how important are all the Chelsea players, old and new, to true supporters.

I hope I can come back many times to relive the fantastic memories with my Chelsea 'family'. Many have been supporting the club long before my time and have many more memories, good and bad, as this book shows. I hope you like it, because you play your part in the history as much as any player does.

All of us – players, directors, managers – are passing through a football club. Supporters are there always. And they never forget.

All the best, always,

Introduction by Rick Glanvill

The history of our club is among the richest and most colourful in the league. Chelsea Football Club has turned heads ever since it changed the football map in 1905–06. In that debut season a northern newspaper, desperate for any titbit for its readers about London's glamorous new visitors, placed an excited note in its stop press section: 'The Chelsea team are now enjoying a luncheon of roast mutton and dry toast.'

Over many years there was plenty of meat, quite a lot of sauce, but only occasional butter for the toast in the form of cups and titles. In contrast the last few years have brought previously undreamt of success. Chelsea has become the best team in Britain, if not Europe. Whatever its fortunes, England's fifth-best supported team has always written headlines, on and off the pitch, and happily there were photographers, cartoonists, eyewitnesses and journalists to record the events.

This pictorial history is an imperfect attempt to capture the spirit of the club in an accessible form. I have tried to unearth new images and words, and provide fresh insight into the object of our obsession over its 101 years, decade by decade. The book couldn't cover every event or personality, but for those it does, I hope it evokes carefree memories if you were there, and fascination if you were not.

Also by Rick Glanvill

Chelsea FC: The Official Biography, Headline (2005)
Rhapsody in Blue. The Chelsea Dream Team (1996)
The Spirit of Chelsea (1997)
The Chelsea Who's Who (1998)

1905–1910

'They're off!' That's how Frederick Parker, 'godfather' of Chelsea Football Club, its conscience and its honorary financial secretary, as well as its programme editor, announced the arrival of the first ever season of professional football at Stamford Bridge. It was a different world then, of course. Professionalism was new, Highbury and Old Trafford didn't exist, and a judge at the time adjourned a case to ask 'What is a motor car?'

The Chelsea board were wealthy high fliers. Alderman J.T. Mears would turn heads driving his Ford from Richmond to the Bridge, and the intention was to have a similar impact on the football establishment, to have fun and to spend and make money doing it.

Parts of Chelsea's lasting personality were quickly established. Promotion and relegation came swiftly and the club's 'splendid gate-drawing effectively silenced

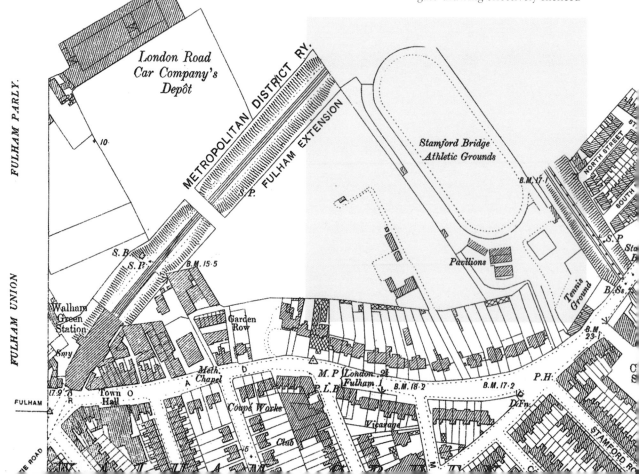

their northern critics', expensive imports (from Scotland, Ireland and Wales) were criticised as overrated, and older rivals hated the unseemly haste of the new club's status and success.

Chelsea's first match at Stamford Bridge was a friendly against Liverpool on Monday 4 September 1905. A contemporary match report recalls an optimistic occasion for the new club. 'Chelsea opened their new ground at Stamford Bridge on Monday evening with a flourish of trumpets, and the pleasing information will be handed down to football posterity that they defeated Liverpool in a "friendly" by four goals to one. This result is a fitting opening tribute, and from the great enclosure nearly eight thousand enthusiasts saw Liverpool overwhelmed … What I liked most about Monday's play was the covering movements and passes of Chelsea's halves.'

The club has the extraordinarily popular stage comedian George Robey (1869–1954) to blame for the 'music hall joke' tag that for many years stopped Chelsea being taken as seriously as the club and its fans would have liked. But it was Norman Long – 'A song, a smile, and a piano' – who immortalised Chelsea's inconsistency in 1933 with his song 'On the Day That Chelsea Went and Won the Cup'.

Apparently Long also dreamed that 'taxi men had change for half a quid', 'lawyers told the truth and then refused to take their fee' and 'the sun came out in Manchester and funny things like that' when 'Chelsea went and won the Final'. Bloomin' cheek.

Now a little while ago I dreamed the most amazing dream.
It tickled me to death when I woke up.
Now you know just how impossible the things we dream of are.
But I dreamed that Chelsea went and won the Cup.
Of course as a result of an astounding thing like this,
A host of other strange events occurred
Norman Long, '*On the Day That Chelsea Went and Won the Cup*' (1933)

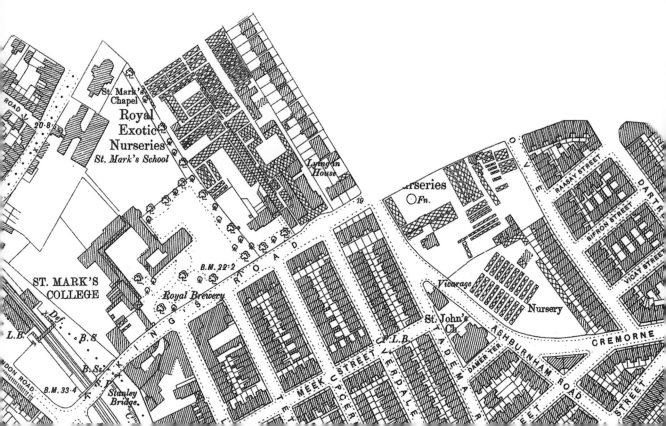

below left Chelsea FC is actually in the borough of Fulham, not Chelsea. More precisely it is in Walham Green, an area never short of watering holes. Here is the scene outside the Underground station in 1904, a year before the club existed. The King's Head (left, now the Slug & Lettuce)

was run by Sam Janes, uncle to Edwin and brother of Alfred, both of whom were publicans, freemasons, and founder directors of the club. The White Hart (centre) survived as a pre-match meet for fans (and players in the 1920s and 30s) until 2005.

below right Walham Green's famous Granville Theatre opened in 1890 and closed as a music hall venue in 1954 with a final performance by G.H. Elliot, 'The Chocolate-Coloured Coon,' followed by speeches and the singing of 'Auld Lang Syne'. It was demolished in the 1990s.

'The list of artists who appeared at the Granville includes all the great names of the turn of the century and many also of recent years, from Marie Lloyd, Little Tich, and Chirgwin, the White-Eyed Kaffir, to George Robey, who gave one of his last performances here, Billy Bennett and Miss Gracie Fields.'   The Times (1954)

left The leading comedian of his day, George Robey, posing in his Chelsea kit, *circa* 1907.

'*Following the sudden death of Chelsea's Scottish international trainer, Jimmy Miller, Robey organized and played in a match early in 1907, between Chelsea and an All Star XI, to help the widow. So well did Robey perform that after the match he was signed on as an amateur. The club having won promotion to the First Division of the Football League, George would say in his act, "I just wanted to make sure that Chelsea stay in the First Division." This was the first known occasion on which the club was mentioned on the music hall stage.*'

Bryan Horsnell, quoted in *George Robey* by Peter Cotes (1972)

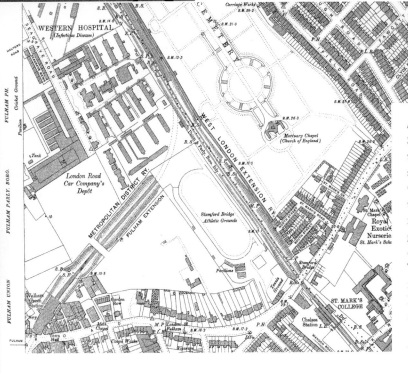

left The 'footprint' of the modern Stamford Bridge, recognisable in this 1893 Ordnance Survey map showing the then London Athletics Club's home, covers almost exactly three fields that were present in the mid-1800s, owned by market gardener John Stunt and sold to developer H.A. 'Gus' Mears in 1904. The site was superbly situated on a main road heading west from central London. Note also Chelsea railway station (bottom right) and Walham Green (now Fulham Broadway) tube station (bottom left).

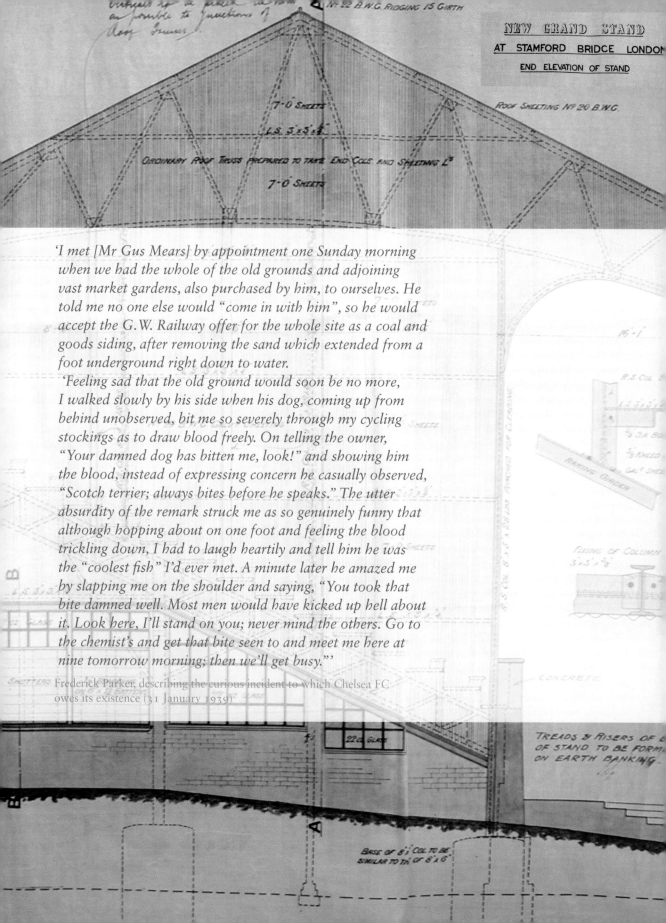

'I met [Mr Gus Mears] by appointment one Sunday morning when we had the whole of the old grounds and adjoining vast market gardens, also purchased by him, to ourselves. He told me no one else would "come in with him", so he would accept the G.W. Railway offer for the whole site as a coal and goods siding, after removing the sand which extended from a foot underground right down to water.

'Feeling sad that the old ground would soon be no more, I walked slowly by his side when his dog, coming up from behind unobserved, bit me so severely through my cycling stockings as to draw blood freely. On telling the owner, "Your damned dog has bitten me, look!" and showing him the blood, instead of expressing concern he casually observed, "Scotch terrier; always bites before he speaks." The utter absurdity of the remark struck me as so genuinely funny that although hopping about on one foot and feeling the blood trickling down, I had to laugh heartily and tell him he was the "coolest fish" I'd ever met. A minute later he amazed me by slapping me on the shoulder and saying, "You took that bite damned well. Most men would have kicked up hell about it. Look here, I'll stand on you; never mind the others. Go to the chemist's and get that bite seen to and meet me here at nine tomorrow morning; then we'll get busy."'

Frederick Parker, describing the curious incident to which Chelsea FC owes its existence (31 January 1939)

'It is Mr Mears' intention to bring together a very strong team, and to apply for admission to the First or Second Division of the Southern League*. Mr Mears intends to transform the Stamford Bridge Grounds, and erect a grand stand designed for the accommodation of 5,000 people. He states that he will be able to find room for no less than 100,000 people! Mr Mears would have it be known that he is acting in the best spirit of the sportsman. We imagine, however, that he also has a keen eye to the shekels. His commercial instinct is too pronounced for "my Englishman's love of sport" to pass muster without a genial addendum.'

Fulham Chronicle (16 December 1904)

*When this strategy was blocked by Henry Norris of Fulham, who had failed to agree terms in 1905 on occupying the new Stamford Bridge, Chelsea applied successfully to the rival Football League instead.

below This photo of an athletics meeting in the spring of 1905 shows the stadium architect Archibald Leitch's east stand close to completion.

'From conception to inauguration, the new Stamford Bridge would be ready for use in eight months.'   Simon Inglis, *Engineering Archie* (2005)

ARCH⁰ LEITCH M.I. MECH. E.
53 VICTORIA STREET
WESTMINSTER, S.W.

'My family are, I believe, unsung heroes in
the Chelsea story. To start with, they ran many
of the watering holes in the area, including the
Rising Sun, where the club was born in 1905.

'Grandfather Edwin, its proprietor, would wake up at 11
every morning to a glass of champagne. He would drink 18
pints of bitter during the morning session, have a lie down in
the afternoon to sleep it off, and then consume another 18 in
the evening. Grandfather loved his sport, so it was natural that
he would get involved in the establishment of the football club
over the road. Supporters know all about the Mearses, but I think
my family's influence in Chelsea's early history went a lot further
than people appreciate. For instance, we have a letter indicating
that quite early on Edwin signed a huge personal cheque to
bail out the club when it was in desperate financial straits – I
think they would not have been able to pay wages without it.
'Edwin died around 1918, but Alfred remained a club director
well into the 1920s, and Elizabeth Janes kept the Duke's Head
[now the Duke on the Green], Parsons Green, for many years,
serving and celebrating with generations of Chelsea fans.'

Michael Janes, grandson of founder-director Edwin Janes (2006)

opposite Chelsea's first board of directors was sports-mad and heavy-drinking, but a high-powered and entrepreneurial one. Pictured in 1908, left to right, they were (back row) George Schomberg, Mayfair saddlemaker, David Calderhead, secretary-manager, Edwin Hurford Janes, publican; (front row) Frederick William Parker, financial secretary, Joseph Theophilus Mears, contractor, Henry Augustus Mears, contractor, Tom Lewin Kinton, wharf manager to the Mearses, John Henry Maltby, solicitor, Henry Boyer, contractor, the Mearses' brother in law. Absent is Alfred Frederick Janes, licensed victualler, and uncle of Edwin.

above This 1905 director's medal, a commemorative gift to founders of the club, is a typical official Chelsea FC item in that it contains a riddle: of all the designs the club could choose for itself, why a civic coat of arms, especially when it has always 'lived' in Fulham rather than the borough of Chelsea, whose heraldry it adopted? The club also adopted the civic motto *Nisi Dominus Frustra*, which means 'Nothing without God' and not, as some may imagine, 'Nothing if not inconsistent.'

'My grandfather John Maltby was head clerk to Chelsea's solicitors, Powell & Rogers, in 1905 and was a director of the club for nearly 20 years. He was born in 1865 and grew up on Green Street, Chelsea, an only child brought up by his mother. His son, my father, Edgar, always said he was a distant father, typical Victorian, and a very heavy drinker. Grandfather lived on Epirus Road and would frequent many of the pubs around Fulham and Chelsea.

'Dad said he knew when it was time to go home because the tail on the "Red Lion" would be waving!

'My dad became very religious, a Baptist, though, and didn't approve of his father's lifestyle at all. He used to try to steer him clear of pubs, or find him to take him home. It's funny, but Dad would have been about 12 when Chelsea was founded, and you would imagine it was an exciting thing for him, but he never mentioned it apart from saying he was given some of the club's old footballs to play with in his garden.'

Hazel Cook (née Maltby), granddaughter of John Henry Maltby (2006)

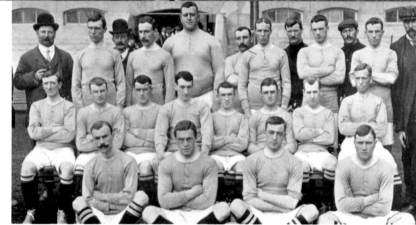

above With a brand new ground and a brand new star-studded team (*right*) football supporters in west London awaited the start of the 1905–06 league season with high excitement.

First League Match
Stockport County 1 Chelsea 0
2 September 1905

'Foulke stood in the goal with his twenty stone of lusty manhood, McEwan was in front of him, and McRoberts at centre-half. Forward there were Copeland and Kirwan, of Tottenham's Cup-winning eleven. To beat such an opposition was a notable beginning for Stockport, especially as Foulke played as well as ever. "As active as a cat," the crowd said, and his nimbleness was indeed astonishing.'

Manchester Guardian (4 September 1905)

Chelsea's first ever league win was recorded in the next match on 9 September 1905 at Blackpool, 1-0, and Hull City were slaughtered 5-1 at home two days later.

left Chelsea's first boss – or player-secretary-manager to set out his full club role – was the Scotsman John Tait Robertson, known as 'Jackie'. 'In the whole long history of football,' he wrote during his first season, 'no club has rushed into fame with such sensational suddenness as Chelsea.' Robertson scored Chelsea's first-ever league goal (the winner away at Blackpool in September 1905) and built a stellar squad that in its second year achieved its aim of promotion to the top flight. But he had already jumped ship to Glossop in November 1906, and so the promotion medals went to stand-in manager Bill Lewis, who himself made way for another Scot, David Calderhead, at the end of the 1906–07 season. Calderhead would become Chelsea's longest-serving manager.

FIXTURES AND SCORING
FIRST TEAM.

Name of Club.		
1905.		
Sept. 2	Stockport	Away
,, 4	Liverpool (F)	Home
,, 9	Blackpool	Away
,, 11	Hull City	Home
,, 16	Bradford City	Away
,, 23	W. Bromwich A.	Home
,, 30	Leicester Fosse	Away
Oct. 7 (E.C.)	1st Grenadier Guards	Home
,, 14	Lincoln City	Away
,, 21	Chesterfield	Home
,, 28 (E.C.)	Burslem *1 · 0*	
,, 30	Port Vale	Away
Nov. 4	Barnsley	Home
,, 6	Everton (F)	Home
,, 11	Clapton Orient	Away
,, 18 (E.C.)	Burnley	Home
,, 25	Leeds City	Away
Dec. 2	Burton United	Home
,, 9 (E.C.)	Grimsby	Home
,, 16	Gainsboro' Trinity	Away
,, 23	Bristol City	Home
,, 25	Manchester U.	Away
,, 26	Glossop	Away
,, 30	Stockport	Home

(handwritten: South. Utd)

'*My work has not been without its amusing side. Amongst the many applications I received was one from a man who said he was a splendid centre-forward, but if that position was not vacant he could manipulate a turnstile. Another wrote, "You will be astonished to see me skip down the line like a deer." A third was willing to "be linesman, goal-keep, or mind the coats".*'   John Tait Robertson (1905)

opposite William Foulke was undoubtedly the main attraction of Chelsea's brand new 'team of experts' as *Cheshire County News* described them. Six foot 2 inches tall and 22 stone, he had the oversize personality to match. Foulke only stayed one season, but his place in Chelsea legend is assured.

'At one Yorkshire town we were met by a group of sandwichmen bearing boards, "Come to —— and see Foulke, the 24½ stones Chelsea goalkeeper." Bill generally "palled" up with me in away games, and when he saw the boards he said to me as he put down his bag (each man carried his own kit in those days), "Thaat's too bad. Watch me give them a fright." Raising his voice to a fierce bellow he shouted, "Twenty-fower stone? I'll give ye twenty-fower stone!" then shuffled his feet as though running after them. The nearest man ran for his life, while Foulke chuckled and quietly resumed his walk. For all his size and strength Foulke, except on very rare occasions, was as gentle as a child in manner.'

Letter written by Frederick Parker (31 January 1939)

below Twenty thousand fans turned up at the Bridge for Chelsea's next Second Division game against West Bromwich Albion, decided by first signing Bob McRoberts' goal.

opposite While on Good Friday, 13 April 1906, Chelsea played host to Manchester United for the first time ever in a promotion decider that Chelsea needed to win. It finished 1-1 in front of an astonishing record

attendance of 67,000, Peddie scoring for United with McDermott equalising in the last few minutes. The first match between the two, at Clayton four months earlier, also finished honours even, 0-0.

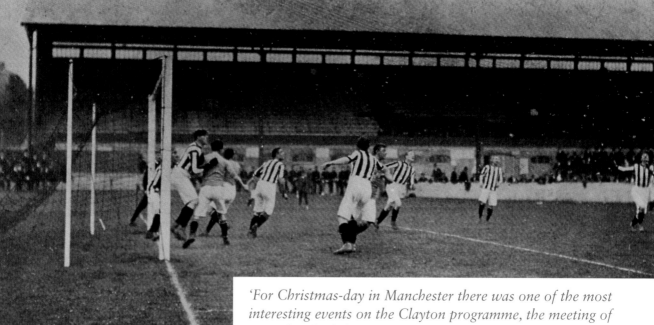

'For Christmas-day in Manchester there was one of the most interesting events on the Clayton programme, the meeting of United and Chelsea. When the fixtures were arranged Chelsea were of course a club of unknown strength.

'Their team has proved brilliantly successful, and they came to Manchester yesterday having been beaten only three times in 17 matches

and having had fewer goals scored against them than any team in the whole League. Such visitors proved an irresistible draw, and the United ground has very seldom been so thronged as Chelsea made it. The match was a glorious and memorable struggle, and its spectators were on the tip-toe of expectation from the first whistle to the last. Chelsea retired unbeaten once more, and with no further addition to their

wonderful "goals against" record, for not a goal was scored
by either side. A few minutes before the end a goal seemed
coming at last, for amid a yell that must have shaken the
chimney towers that circle the ground the referee summoned
the mighty Foulke to a penalty ordeal. Chelsea had played
gloriously, but no one doubted that they were doomed now.
Bonthron took the kick, and sensitive people stopped their
ears as he moved. *Alas! for United.*

No yell followed. In trying to shoot wide of Foulke's twenty
stones he sent the ball wide of the post, and the chance was
gone. A draw was a just result. Chelsea were the more artistic,
the more polished, and the more accurate side – no eleven of
finer "class" has been to Manchester this season.'

Manchester Guardian (26 December 1905)

below With the maximum wage in place, Chelsea's 'added extras', ranging from access to state-of-the-art medical treatment to trips abroad, helped lure the best players. So Chelsea players were soon well travelled – from Bognor Regis to Copenhagen. The three players wearing comical false moustaches here at Bognor could include Geordie Key and George Hilsdon (on the right) and are likely to have been pictured before the FA Cup game with Lincoln City in January 1907.

'It was a highly distinguished audience led by HRH Prince Valdemar which turned up last Sunday [for Chelsea v the 'Stævnet']. The whole stand was fully occupied and outside the rope people stood five or six deep following play with the utmost interest.

'As expected, this match turned out to be the biggest yet of the tournament.

'True, the Danes lost and by quite a margin, but this does not reflect the balance of play, as at least two of the six goals scored by the English were decidedly offside, a fact which was also admitted by Chelsea themselves.

'The two English teams played last Monday evening in an exceedingly interesting and exciting match as a finale for the football tournament.

'As expected from a meeting between two such talented clubs, it turned out to be a highly interesting and informative match. Against all expectations Southampton managed a victory 2-1. Chelsea's type of game is typically full of short-passing, and the weakness in this lies in the lack of speed combined with a great deal of passing the ball back to the half-backs that opponents, once they are familiar with it, very often two out of three times manage to get back in defence and thereby hinder the attackers in scoring a goal.

'This was not understood by the Danish defence but fully exploited by Southampton who thus, with the help of their excellent goalkeeper, won the match.'

Danish newspaper *Idraetten* (1906)

above Chelsea's tour of Copenhagen in June 1906, sponsored by the local club B.93, quickly established the tradition of summer globetrotting. They beat a local 'stævnet' or representative side 6-2, then played fellow tourists Southampton.

'The huge amorphous crowd [at Stamford Bridge], 30,000 or 40,000 strong, is an amazing phenomenon. Quite half of it is composed of pale, weedy lads, who ought to be playing football themselves. Unfortunately there is not room for them to play, though the London County Council, the Playing Fields Society, and other public authorities are doing what is possible to extend the accommodation. The poor fellows are chiefly drawn from the vast brick-and-mortar ambuscades* of Fulham, Wandsworth, and further Westward and Southward – parts of London much more dreary and monotonous than the East-end of 20 years ago. It is better on the whole that they should spend their Saturday afternoons playing football by proxy than in their mean, monotonous streets. After all professional football has its uses, and if it kept to the letter of the rules the game would provide invaluable object lessons in discipline.'

A Special Correspondent, *The Times* (19 October 1907)

* Places of ambush, i.e. where a person is likely to get mugged

below The Beefeater gin distillery on Cale Street, Chelsea, was a large employer as well as a symbol of local vice hidden among the well-to-do streets of the borough. Many of those who went to Chelsea's first matches would have worked there five and a half days a week.

below left Gin workers gather outside the factory before heading off on a works outing in 1904.

Season tickets were priced to attract the masses in 1905. An old-fashioned 'guinea' (£1/1s) for men to watch all 38 home league games from the stand represented good value when a joiner could earn around £2 a week. Women, whose average weekly wage was only 7 shillings, and 'boys' paid half that (10s/6d), as did men who watched from the simple banking surrounding the pitch. The strategy worked. On Good Friday 1906 Stamford Bridge set a new league attendance record of 67,000 for the visit of Manchester United. Even that was surpassed on 27 December 1909 as Chelsea beat champions Newcastle 2-1.

But buying a team befitting such a following came at a price.

'Football [has] indeed bounded into big proportions, for we find eight clubs, including Tottenham Hotspur and Woolwich Arsenal, have, in "gates", taken over £10,000. The reverse side of the picture is shown in the clubs which have sustained a loss. We now know to what extent Chelsea was prepared to bid for First Division honours, for their loss, despite making such a bold bid for promotion, is given as the sum of £5,000 [approx. half a million pounds in today's money]. It is difficult to estimate the attendances at Stamford Bridge but, after their record crowd on the occasion of the first visit of Manchester United last Good Friday, the loss staggered us.'

The Goal Post (14 August 1906)

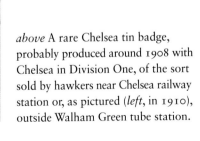

above A rare Chelsea tin badge, probably produced around 1908 with Chelsea in Division One, of the sort sold by hawkers near Chelsea railway station or, as pictured (*left*, in 1910), outside Walham Green tube station.

Chelsea's first spell in the second tier was short-lived. After 1905–06's near-miss, Jackie Robertson was temporarily replaced as manager by secretary Bill Lewis, who steered the all-star squad to promotion at the second attempt.

Promisingly, that 1906–07 season opened with a sensational 9-2 win over Glossop (*below*) and the unearthing of a legend as new signing George Hilsdon scored five of the goals. David Calderhead led the new boys in the top flight

but the price of the board's aspirations soon became clear. Ravaged by injuries, Chelsea were relegated, to the glee of many rival clubs and despite desperate spring buys, in 1910.

'Chelsea did splendidly, and it is clear that their forwards have the happy knack of finding the net. Nine goals to two is a tremendous victory, and the pity of it is that Chelsea had to nurse their injured goalkeeper [Byrne]. In making a fine save of a long shot he injured his arm and will be out of the field for two or three weeks. The attendance at Stamford Bridge exceeded 14,000, and the club should run comfortably on such figures.'

The Goal Post, Chelsea 9 Glossop 2, match report (4 September 1906)

left After promotion, despite five defeats in the first six matches and the anchor position in the First Division, at least 35,000 turned up to see the Pensioners lose 1-3 at home to fellow strugglers Bolton on 12 October. Enthusiasm didn't wane, and the rot stopped after this match as Chelsea finished mid-table. Note the spectators perched on advertising hoardings for a better vantage point.

right The England team in Glasgow 1908. In the front row (second right to left) are future team-mates Jimmy Windridge, Vivian Woodward and George Hilsdon. (Incidentally, fourth from the left at the back is half-back Ben Warren.) When England beat Wales 7-1 on 16 March that year, Woodward scored three, Hilsdon two and Windridge one. Between 1909 and 1911, all three figured in Chelsea's star-studded forward line.

'In the internationals [of 1908] George Hilsdon was at centre, and Vivian Woodward at inside-right. I have often been asked which of the two I preferred.

'Candour compels me to say that, in my opinion, George Hilsdon was superior to Woodward as centre, and Woodward was better at inside-right. To my way of thinking the famous amateur [Woodward] was too gentle for centre-forward duties. He was a wonderful shot, knew how to keep his wings together, and knew positional play, but lacked the fire of Hilsdon.'

Jimmy Windridge, *Sports Pictures* (11 March 1922)

'During Chelsea's first season the player-manager, John Tait Robertson, made a chance discovery destined to have immense influence on the club's fortunes. Going to a Fulham v West Ham Reserves match to see another player, Robertson was at once struck by the form of a 19-year-old inside-left playing for the same team, declaring the lad should make an ideal centre-forward, and resolving to obtain him if possible at the end of the season.

  'Player's name was George Hilsdon. Put straight into Chelsea's League eleven, at centre-forward, for the opening match of the season, Hilsdon scored five goals which must surely be a record for any player making his league debut. Within a month he had been given his first cap – to score a hat-trick against Ireland in the Inter-League game at Belfast.'

Letter written by Frederick Parker (31 January 1939)

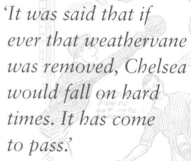

After the Hilsdon weathervane (*left*) was removed in 1972, Chelsea suffered relegations in 1975 and 1979. A replica from the 1980s now resides above the East Stand.

'It was said that if ever that weathervane was removed, Chelsea would fall on hard times. It has come to pass.'

Geoffrey Green, *The Times*, 1982

'Growing up I was always aware of what a star my grandfather had been for Chelsea. My father – also George, of course – always said "Gatling Gun" really enjoyed his time at Stamford Bridge – perhaps a little too much at the end, when he sought solace in drink a bit. He also said that when the idea of a statue came up in 1908 [opposite, far right], Gatling Gun was dead set against it. He was a modest man and felt it would be far too ostentatious. Luckily the England cap he earned in 1907 to become Chelsea's first England international [opposite] stayed in the family.'

George Hilsdon, grandson of 'Gatling Gun' (2006)

'Hilsdon, the Chelsea dasher, is thin and light, but very fast indeed, and the way he meets centres to send them home gee-whizz is delightful from a spectacular point of view.'

The Goal Post (14 August 1906)

CHELSEA'S FIRST GOAL – HILSDON BEATS FOULKE

M. HAMILTON

left On 15 September 1906 Chelsea played Bradford City in a league match. This cartoon from *The Goal Post* tells the story of the match in which Chelsea put five goals past former keeper Willie Foulke on his first visit to Stamford Bridge since his summer transfer. Chelsea's goals came from McDermott, Copeland (2), Moran and George 'Gatling Gun' Hilsdon.

In six years at Stamford Bridge centre-forward George Hilsdon scored 107 goals, including six in an FA Cup match against Worksop and five in a league match against Glossop – still Chelsea's record wins. He top-scored for the club for three successive seasons, 1906–09, on his way to becoming the club's first terrace legend. Such was his form in 1908 that *Chat* magazine ran a competition for its readers to design a statue in his honour intended to be erected inside the Stamford Bridge gates – one of the prize-winning entries is shown (*above*). Unfortunately, the club did not adopt the idea. But it is said that the weathervane which has topped one of the stands at Stamford Bridge for many years now was modelled on George Hilsdon.

A great dribbler and goalscorer and one of Chelsea's first signings in 1905, Jimmy Windridge scored 58 goals in 152 games. This dramatic illustration captures the moment on 18 December 1909 when his goal helped the Blues win the first-ever derby with Spurs, 2-1, at the Bridge.

In April 1910, with seven key players, including Hilsdon, unavailable, and relegation looming, the board splashed out desperately on four new players, including Bob Whittingham (*below left*), a consistent marksman who would serve Chelsea for 11 years. Chelsea were still relegated. However, one of the big transfer coups of Chelsea's early years was the nabbing of the most renowned forward of his day, amateur international Vivian Woodward (*below right*), from London rivals Chelmsford earlier that season. In its day, it was as sensational a signing as that of Gallacher, Gullit or Shevchenko.

'There was many a glad smile round the regions of Stamford Bridge when it was announced that Vivian J. Woodward had thrown in his lot with the Chelsea Club. Possibly Chelsea never have had such a slice of luck.

'I should say that without a doubt Vivian Woodward is the most popular man in football today. Popular with players, popular with the spectators wherever and whenever he plays, he owes his unique position chiefly to one thing. First, foremost, and all the time he is a gentleman. He may play well or he may play moderately (he never plays badly), but no matter how he plays his very presence in a team is ever a great factor of success. He inspires his men with his unflagging energy. He inspires a confidence in them as no other player could ever do.'

Chelsea Chronicle (1909)

left Gus Mears's spending spree in 1909–10 was intended to help the club avoid relegation. The move did not meet with approval and many in football were pleased when it failed. However, the 'moneybags' tag that was tarred to the club's name as a result has stuck ever since.

'Had the great Vivian been a professional player his transfer fee, I fancy, would have been something near a record one. Instead Woodward comes to us for love, and we may take it that he is already the idol of Stamford Bridge.'

Chelsea Chronicle (1909)

1911–1920

The 'war to end all wars' left its mark on this decade in a way that didn't seem possible at its optimistic start. Chelsea were promoted again in 1912 and this time established a firm foothold in England's top tier that would last 12 years. Four of those were under wartime restrictions, during which Chelsea remained a huge attraction to fans as well as to several famous enlisted players, who 'guested' for the Pensioners and helped earn some silverware.

Before that, though, the club was the victim of a match-fixing scandal, made its FA Cup semi-final debut, then the final, and boasted a first big overseas superstar alongside popular, emerging home-growns.

Chelsea's first FA Cup final, however, was a disappointment. The match, against Sheffield United,

was switched from London to Manchester and the Blades' 3-0 victory was witnessed by very few Chelsea fans. The *Manchester Guardian*'s match report makes depressing reading. 'The conditions in which the game was played were almost sepulchral. A run of fine, clear days was succeeded by a typical Manchester drizzle accompanied by a clammy fog. At the beginning of the second half the fog was so dense that spectators of the one side had only the haziest notion of what was happening on the other. There was a crowd of over 50,000 present. It included numbers of men in uniform – and a much larger number of men who ought to have been in uniform. In the lower rows of the stand there was a group of wounded soldiers, accompanied by their nurses. There never was a cup final played in such a depressing atmosphere. A sombre consciousness of war overhung the crowd, and the final touch was added when the band started to play hymns.'

After the war the league proper returned on the first day of September 1919. Amazingly, the Chelsea team showed just five changes from April 1915. The six who'd played in Chelsea's last official league match were stalwarts Bettridge, Jack Harrow, Laurence Abrams, Harold Halse and keeper James Molyneux, now well into his 30s and under pressure from understudy Colin Hampton, a war hero who'd received the Military Medal for Gallantry in Mesopotamia.

In 1911, an FA Cup run arrived like a forgotten dream, with Chelsea making it all the way to the semi-finals in front of huge crowds.

'Stamford Bridge presented a wonderful appearance half an hour before the start of the cup tie, over 65,000 being present. Twenty minutes from the start, from a centre from the right, Whittingham scored and, five minutes later, from a cross by Hilsdon, he again beat Skiller. With ten minutes to go, Chelsea settled matters, Bridgeman scoring from Douglas's centre. Result: Chelsea 3 Swindon 1.'

The Scotsman, FA Cup quarter-final match report (13 March 1911)

left Second Division Chelsea's first-ever semi-final ended with a below par 0-3 defeat to Newcastle, who lost to Bradford in the final. Promotion the following season eased the pain, and four years later Chelsea beat the same team en route to their first final appearance with a goal by New King's Road schoolboy Harry Ford.

'The attendance at St Andrew's, Birmingham, reached only 34,000. It was a disappointing game, Newcastle holding the upper hand from start to finish, and it is difficult to account for the feeble display given by the southern team.

'The balance of the forward line was probably upset by the absence of Hilsdon, for whom Vivian Woodward made a very indifferent substitute, but the team as a whole played very much below the form which carried them to the semi-final.'

The Scotsman, FA Cup semi-final match report (27 March 1911)

below These rare medallions produced to commemorate Chelsea's return to the top flight in 1912 after just two seasons are interesting for two reasons. Firstly, because the more elaborate one is for board members, and the simpler one for the men who did the work, the players. Secondly, that they feature a cipher-style badge formed from the initials 'CFC' – a design that replaced the earlier one featuring Chelsea borough's coat of arms – which was not widely known to have been used until the late-1940s.

right The sensitivity of this illustration from the *Chelsea Handbook* for 1912–13 leaves something to be desired – the *Titanic* had sunk midway through Chelsea's successful promotion run-in just a few months earlier, with immense loss of life – but the message is clear: watch out for potential First Division menaces, depicted here as icebergs, and avoid relegation at all cost. At the helm is popular skipper and Scotland international full-back 'Jock' Cameron, soon to lose his place to Jimmy Sharp.

Pensioner (to Captain Cameron at the Wheel)
" Now, my boy, steer clear of these icebergs, some of 'em look dangerous, and we don't want another disaster."

1 November 1913. It's 15 minutes
before kick-off on the day Chelsea
host Middlesbrough in Division
One, captured for posterity by an
anonymous photographer using a
plate camera. An omnibus trundles
past the parade of shops on the right
(still there), including the Rising
Sun pub, run by Chelsea FC director
Alfred Janes. Perhaps that's the
landlord's wife, peering over the
balcony onto the throng below,
where a shop offers to store fans'
bikes. An attendance of 40,000 is
recorded on this day and the huge

queue can be seen snaking back over the railway bridge. More people emerge at the back on the right from the Chelsea and Fulham railway station. Police maintain space for the cars and cabs of wealthier supporters in front of the stadium's wonderful old arched gates, topped then by flags, as an omnibus ambles past on its way to north London. The building behind the gates was lost in the Chelsea Village development, but the tall mansion block behind stands to this day. Chelsea won the match 3-2.

below In December 1913 a goal from Harry Halse earned a welcome draw at home to champions Sunderland. This photo captures the moment after a free kick from five yards out, given against goalie Molyneux for 'carrying the ball', was repelled by defenders on the line. Nils Middelboe (left), playing his fourth game for the Blues, uses his telescopic leg to block the resulting shot from Charlie Buchan. Moly, stranded in the centre, stands ahead of the rest of his team (left to right: Halse, Vivian Woodward, Bob Whittingham, George Hunter, Billy Bridgeman, Walter Bettridge and Jimmy Sharp). They all lined up along the goalmouth for the free kick, representing probably the most expensive wall constructed at Stamford Bridge. Chelsea's talented side finished the season in its highest top league position so far: eighth.

below The 1912–13 season saw the Pensioners desperately staving off relegation again. One controversial match towards the end of the season saw Chelsea beat mid-table Liverpool 2-1, causing Woolwich Arsenal chairman Henry Norris (the former Fulham chairman whose nose was put out of joint by Chelsea's success) to cry foul. Norris's misfiring Gunners were relegated. Chelsea stayed up.

'*The joint commission of the Football Association and the Football League appointed to inquire into allegations by Mr H.G. Norris as to the conduct of certain Liverpool players in the match [at] Chelsea on 24 March [1913] sat yesterday. After the meeting the following report was drawn up and issued to the Press, "The commission is satisfied that no inducement was offered to the Liverpool players to influence the result of the match. There is evidence that the form displayed by Liverpool players was unsatisfactory, but the commission is satisfied that the allegation that they did not desire to win the match is unfounded. Mr Norris admitted that he was indiscreet in giving publicity to his statement instead of reporting to the Football Association and the Football League."*' The Times (12 April 1913)

'During the whole period Chelsea have been in the First League I can only recollect two instances where they have finished up in anything like the position their followers have a right to expect, viz., third in 1919–20, and eighth, I think, in 1913–14. This latter season was only a second-half revival, and the reward for bringing young players to the front. I am aware that the club has until this season [1921–22] had good runs in the Cup from 1914–15 onwards, but surely with their resources a decent position in the league ought to be attainable. The whole trouble is lack of enterprise, and a contentment with just being a league club.'

Letter from 'South-west,' of Earlsfield (4 March 1922)

right Chelsea produced one of English football's early overseas stars when they signed the 6-foot-2-inch Denmark international Nils Middelboe in 1913. Middelboe, cosmopolitan Chelsea's first foreign international, made his debut as skipper in front of 40,000 at the Bridge against Derby on 13 November and, as an amateur, always emphatically refused match expenses, saying, 'Oh! No, no, no! It cost me only three pence for a bus.' He stayed for nine years and later, as a director of FC Copenhagen, always maintained a kinship with the Blues. Middelboe scored the first-ever goal at the Olympics in 1908.

right An early example, from 1913–14, of press scorn aimed at poor old Chelsea. Inconsistent, and bottom of the table at the time, the Pensioners were seen as a 'yo-yo' club – always up and down between First and Second Divisions – having sprung to fame so quickly and spent so much money on players.

PITY THE POOR PENSIONER.

BLACKBURN - R
TOTTENHAM - H
W. BROMWICH - A
MANCHESTER - U
BOLTON - W
EVERTON
BRADFORD - C
SUNDERLAND
DERBY Co
MANCHESTER - C
OLDHAM - A
SHEFFIELD - W
BURNLEY
LIVERPOOL
NEWCASTLE - U
MIDDLESBORO'
ASTON VILLA
SHEFFIELD - U
PRESTON - N-E
CHELSEA.   RESERVED

SPARE A POINT PLEASE

BACK ON HIS OLD PITCH.

'The manager [David Calderhead, pictured below], as I knew him 25–30 years ago, was rather impersonal regarding his relationship with the players. He only showed up in the dressing room a few times and didn't mix with the players very much, not more than necessary. Sometimes he viewed the training, which was controlled by the trainer, and only by the trainer. There were no tactical meetings with the manager, as this was not something that was known about at that time.'

Nils Middelboe (1944)

right Chelsea's first FA Cup final appearance was a huge anticlimax for the few supporters who were able to overcome travel problems getting to Old Trafford, Manchester, chosen to avoid absenteeism. So many servicemen inhabited the terraces that it was dubbed the 'Khaki Cup Final'. Chelsea, skippered by Fred Taylor (shaking hands, left) and dogged by key injuries, were in disarray. But in a typically generous gesture, Vivian Woodward, back on leave from the front, refused to take regular marksman Bob Thomson's place when it was offered. The weather reflected the solemn mood. Chelsea lost 3-0.

POST OFFICE
TELEGRAPHS

E241 2-0 WIMBLEDON PARK SWB 18

TAYLOR CAPTAIN CHELSEA CLUB OLD TRAFFORD GROUND MANCHESTER

GOOD LUCK MUST WIN OR SNOW USE

POST OFFICE
TELEGRAPHS

BILL AND SIDFORD

'The Chelsea [forwards'] attempts at combined zig-zag movements were mercilessly broken up by the swift and decisive counter-attacks of the Sheffield halves and full-backs, and so clever a centre as Thomson was for the most part vainly shadowing a ball that he rarely touched. On the other half of the line the position was exactly the reverse. The Sheffield forwards, in age, tactics, and staying power, were as palpably superior to the Chelsea defence as their own defence was to the Chelsea forward line.'

Manchester Guardian (26 April 1915)

below Harry Ford was a local lad who delighted fans with his pace, skill and cutting-in down the right flank in the years before the First World War. When he returned from war duty, the paper *All Sports* was confident he could reproduce the 'scintillating' form he showed before. In all, Ford stayed 12 years a player and was always a frequent visitor to the Bridge for the greyhound racing.

'I don't know how true it is but he was supposed to be the finest outside-right Chelsea ever had. He wasn't really very well paid. He was on £6 a week, £4 in the summer, something like that. When he left Chelsea he came out with nothing. They didn't give the players anything like they did later. When he finished football he had to go in the building trade as a painter and decorator for the rest of his life. He used to like the greyhounds at Stamford Bridge too. Unfortunately the family was so poor at one stage that he had to pawn his 1915 runners-up medal. He always expected to get the money to buy it back because it meant a lot to him, but he was never able to.

'Chelsea didn't really keep in contact with him. But when they were in the finals, in 1967 and 1970, I used to write to them, tell 'em who I was and they'd send tickets for me and my husband.'

Gladys Hunt, Harry Ford's daughter (2005)

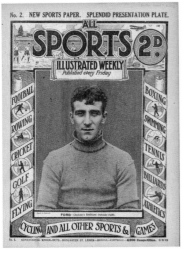

'On Saturday and yesterday recruiting appeals were made to gatherings of young men in London and the provinces. Saturday's efforts were directed to the crowds which were present at football matches, and the results were grievously disappointing. There is apparently something about the professional football match spectator which makes a recruiting appeal failure. At the Chelsea ground Colonel Burn, MP, was one of the speakers. Recruiting sergeants were present – but not a man was induced to join. At other football grounds appeals were made, and with equal ill-success.'

The Times (23 November 1914)

above The attacks on football's 'unpatriotic loafers' struck home. Recruitment drives played on the guilt of those enjoying themselves watching the reduced game while others made the ultimate sacrifice on the field of battle. A new 'footballers' battalion' was formed, the 17th Middlesex.

Many present and former Chelsea players would join up, some – such as Hilsdon (gas inhalation ended his career) and Woodward (front row, third left) – were injured; some, like Harry Wilding (*above right*) and keeper Colin Hampton, were decorated for bravery.

Only two players with Chelsea connections, that we know of, were killed in action. In 1916, former Chelsea inside-right Arthur Wileman was killed on active service. A year later popular onetime Blues keeper Bob 'Pom-Pom' Whiting (*opposite*) suffered the same fate. Ironically, Whiting's nickname came from his ability to launch a goal kick like the latest battlefield howitzer.

'I very much regret to have to inform you that your husband, No. F-74 Private R. Whiting, of this Battalion, was killed in action on the 28th of last month. He was killed instantaneously by shellfire in the recent offensive operations. Will you please accept my sincere sympathy in your loss. Your husband lost his life while attending to the wounded under fire, and died while doing his duty both well and nobly. He is buried very near the scene of the action near Vimy Ridge.'

Extracted from letters dated 15 May 1917, which Whiting's widow received from 2nd Lieutenant J.G. Howard, acting adjutant, and unnamed commanding officer, 'B' Company, 17th Middlesex.

About 400 of the professional football players of London, directors, and other officials of the clubs attended a meeting held in Fulham Town Hall. The meeting was convened by the committee responsible for the formation of the 17th (Football) Battalion of the Middlesex Regiment.

'It was stated that the clubs were prepared to pay the wages of those players who enlisted to the end of the season, that they would be permitted to live at their home until called upon to bear arms, and that they would be released to play in all club matches.

'Mr Joynson-Hicks [MP for Fulham] said that the meeting had not been called to answer attacks made on football. Mr Hayes-Fisher ... believed that [the battalion] would be formed of the pick of British citizens, and at the end of the war would have a magnificent record to its credit. He did not believe that one man in a thousand refused to join the army because he was absorbed in football. That man would not join even if all football were stopped. At the celebrated Chelsea match, of which so much has been said, nearly one-half of the men present were in khaki.

'When the Chief Recruiting Officer for London, appealing as an old football player, asked for recruits, there was an immediate response. Parker (Clapton Orient) led the way, and was followed by Buckley (Bradford), Ford (Chelsea), and Needham (Brighton and Hove Albion). In singles and couples others left their seats, until 35 players had offered themselves.'   The Times (16 December 1914)

In 1915 professional sport ended and the league was regionalised to reduce the demands on travel and scarce fuel resources. In the south-east the London Combination was formed. The dividend for supporters was that locally billeted servicemen were able to turn out for the local teams. One London club manager had scouts out at all the capital's mainline rail stations on the look-out for footballers on leave from the front. Within easy reach of Aldershot, Chelsea benefited more than many other clubs. Wartime guests at the Bridge included Corporal Ted Vizard (*top*) and Bombardier Joe Smith of Bolton (*centre*), the Sunderland star Charles Buchan (*bottom*) (later famous for his *Football Monthly* magazine – a title briefly owned by Chelsea in the 1990s), all England internationals, and David Jack, soon to become one. Others guested anonymously – an 'A.P. Ensioner' played in November 1918 – to evade the attention of beady-eyed officers.

E. T. VIZARD
BOLTON WANDERERS.

J. SMITH
BOLTON WANDERERS.

'I have heard quite a lot about my wartime football with Chelsea. I really don't know where some people get their information from, for I have only played one game for the Pensioners. It was a game I have good cause to remember, for a frost made the ground so hard that it was like playing on concrete.

'I like to keep the ball on the ground when I'm playing, but you can't keep the ball low on hard ground. I don't think I played well, but the Stamford Bridge people must have had a different opinion, for when professional league football was resumed after the war, they sought my services and offered the [Plymouth] Argyle, for whom I signed immediately after being "demobbed", quite a nice cheque.'

David Jack, *Sports Pictures* (25 March 1922)

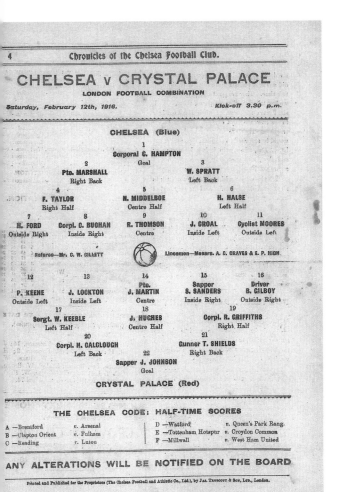

4   **Chronicles of the Chelsea Football Club.**

CHELSEA v CRYSTAL PALACE
LONDON FOOTBALL COMBINATION

Saturday, February 12th, 1916.   **Kick-off 3.30 p.m.**

CHELSEA (Blue)

1
Corporal C. HAMPTON
Goal

2   **3**
Pte. MARSHALL   W. SPRATT
Right Back   Left Back

4   **5**   **6**
F. TAYLOR   N. MIDDELBOE   H. HALSE
Right Half   Centre Half   Left Half

7   **8**   **9**   **10**   **11**
H. FORD   Corpl. C. BUCHAN R. THOMSON   J. CROAL   Cyclist MOORES
Outside Right Inside Right   Centre   Inside Left   Outside Left

Referee—Mr. C. W. GILLETT   Linesmen—Messrs. A. C. GRAVES & E. P. HIGH.

12   **13**   **14**   **15**   **16**
                          Pte.   Sapper   Driver
P. KEENE   J. LOCKTON   J. MARTIN S. SANDERS   B. GILBOY
Outside Left Inside Left   Centre   Inside Right Outside Right

17   **18**   **19**
Sergt. W. KEEBLE   J. HUGHES   Corpl. R. GRIFFITHS
Left Half   Centre Half   Right Half

20   **21**
Corpl. H. CALCLOUGH   Gunner T. SHIELDS
Left Back   Right Back

22
Sapper J. JOHNSON
Goal

CRYSTAL PALACE (Red)

THE CHELSEA CODE: HALF-TIME SCORES

A —Brentford	r. Arsenal	D —Watford	v. Queen's Park Rang.
B —Clapton Orient	r. Fulham	E —Tottenham Hotspur	v. Croydon Common
C —Reading	r. Luton	F —Millwall	v. West Ham United

ANY ALTERATIONS WILL BE NOTIFIED ON THE BOARD

Printed and Published for the Proprietors (The Chelsea Football and Athletic Co., Ltd.), by Jas. Truscott & Son, Ltd., London.

It's a shame some of these 'unofficial' match scorelines against our neighbours don't appear in the record books. In March 1916, for instance, one-eyed marksman Bob Thomson scored seven and Charlie Buchan four in an 11-1 thrashing of Luton Town. A month later Chelsea beat the Arsenal 9-0, with Buchan notching four more and Thomson five. In all Bob Thomson scored 38 goals that season.

Fulham suffered similar treatment at Stamford Bridge as war drew to a close.

'Victory for either side in this match very likely carried the [London Combination] championship with it. Fulham won the toss, and had the driving rain behind them. But from a free kick the Chelsea forwards came away, and Kelly got off alone to centre well.

The ball rebounded to Rolls, who found the net with a smashing drive.

'A few minutes later Kelly again centred and Thomson, springing high in the air, headed a wonderful goal. A fine game followed, with Chelsea more often dangerous. After saving from Rolls, Drabble was beaten by Woodward, who had the easiest job to tip it in the net. Halse promptly put in a fifth goal with a surprise shot from long range. Chelsea led at half-time 5-0. Fulham attacked on resuming, but failed to trouble Hughes, and Thomson had a soft shot close to goal, at which he miskicked, but he shot only inches wide a minute later. At the end Thomson added another, and Chelsea won 7-0.'

Chelsea v Fulham match report, *News of the World* (31 March 1918)

above The Chelsea team that lost 1-0 to Crystal Palace on 12 February 1916 included Corporal Colin Hampton in goal, Private Marshall at right back, Corporal Charlie Buchan at inside right and Cyclist Moores on the left wing. Note the 'Chelsea Code' – half time scores from other matches were displayed next to the relevant letters to keep supporters informed.

-CHELSEA'S LONDON CUP

CHELSEA WIN THE LONDON VICTORY CUP.

Winners Play Fulham at Their Own Game of Importing Talent.

GRAND HALF-BACK PLAY.

(CHELSEA, 3; FULHAM, 0.)

Despite the rain 36,000 people saw Chelsea beat Fulham by 3 goals to 0 in the final of the London Victory Cup at Highbury on Saturday. Chelsea thoroughly deserved their success, but it was not until twenty minutes from the end that they scored their first goal.

Somehow it struck me as a case of poetic justice when Rutherford, of the Arsenal, shot two goals and won the game for Chelsea. It was Fulham that introduced outside talent in this competition. And it was against the Arsenal that Fulham started this match-winning policy.

In addition to Rutherford, who played inside left, Chelsea was assisted by Vizard (Bolton) on the same wing, and Dickie, the Kilmarnock centre half. Whittingham did not turn out for Fulham, who had the Middlesbrough man, Elliott, at centre forward, with Carr, of the same club, on his right.

Quite a feature of the match was the splendid half-back play on both sides. So well did Torrance (centre half) play for Fulham that he was unlucky to be on the losing side. McNeal also was very fine. The fair-haired Scot, Dickie, was splendid for Chelsea, and Middleboe put in a lot of clever work at left half.

RUTHERFORD'S TWO GOALS.

Middleboe's mission was to stop the Fulham attack and to feed Rutherford. The respective centre forwards, Elliott and Wilding, were given but little scope owing to the fine form of the halves. Whitehouse played a great game for Chelsea, and the inside right had a share in all three goals. Bettridge and Harrow, of Chelsea, were the sounder backs.

Without being particularly exciting, play went on even lines in the first half. Early on an accurate centre by Vizard gave Rutherford a chance, but he failed to get in his kick.

Elliott, so closely watched by Dickie, had little scope, and Carr was marksman-in-chief. Just before half-time he brought Molyneux to his knees with a fine drive.

Fulham had the best of the exchanges for a time after resuming. Elliott missed narrowly twice, but his shooting was not great. After twenty-five minutes Rutherford opened the scoring for Chelsea. Wilding put in a centre from the right, and Whitehouse placed the ball for Rutherford to touch it into the net.

Chelsea were now irresistible, and within ten minutes Whitehouse beat McNeal, and sent over a great centre for Rutherford to again dash the ball through. The Fulham defence was somewhat shaky, and just before the finish Wilding added the final goal.   J. F. W.

In 1919 Chelsea – not for the last time – won a knockout competition invented by its own chairman. Thirty thousand people watched the final at Highbury (*above*). Neil, the father of future Blue John Harris, played for Fulham. Jack Rutherford of Arsenal scored two of Chelsea's goals.

'At a special meeting of the London Football Combination, held at Winchester House last night, Mr Claude Kirby, of Chelsea, presiding, it was decided to arrange a London Combination Victory Cup competition. The proceedings of the matches are to be pooled, and a certain percentage to be agreed upon to go to charities. The cup is to become the property of the winners.

'It was also decided that, subject to the approval of the FA, clubs be permitted to allow their players 5s [25p] per week for training (two nights each week) and 15s [75p] per match.'   *Daily News* (7 December 1918)

'Our supporters have, doubtless, followed with great interest the reports of the various important meetings which have been held during the past month relating to "after the war" football ... Chelsea are, at present, suffering a great injustice by being relegated to the Second Division as the direct result of a match which The Football Association, The Football League, one of H.M. Judges, and last, but not least, a British jury have all agreed was "squared."*

'Our supporters may rest assured that the Directors of The Chelsea FC are not allowing the matter to rest, but have, since Monday's meeting, appealed to The Football League Committee to put things right. Our shareholders, members and followers can help considerably by writing to their favourite newspapers emphasising the wrong which will be done if Chelsea have to play in the Second Division next season.'

Chelsea Chronicle (18 January 1919)

*The fixed match was Manchester United v Liverpool on 2 April 1915, which United surprisingly won to leave Chelsea in a relegation slot. Massive betting on the scoreline, 2-0, in the north-west alerted the authorities, and relatives of United's Enoch 'Knocker' West were found to be big beneficiaries by a Football League inquiry. Following the inquiry and a libel action West lost against a magazine that reported the scandal, the League decided against dumping United, but diplomatically expanded the number of teams in the First Division by two – including Chelsea, who increased the capacity of their grandstand by 10,000 in celebration.

On the opening weekend of the new season in September 1919, with Chelsea rightly reinstated in the top tier, 35,000 people watched at Goodison Park as the slickers from the Big Smoke stunned Everton, still reigning Division One champions four years on, with a 3-2 win. In the closing moments of the last league proper, a 2-2 draw at the Bridge had confirmed the Toffeemen as champions.

As late as August 1924 the repercussions of the Great War were still being felt. During a pre-season practice match, Andy Wilson injured the hand of the arm that had been damaged during the conflict. An x-ray showed that a lump of shrapnel remained in his flesh and had to be removed by another operation. Kaiser Bill's bombs meant that he missed the start of the season, six years after hostilities had ceased.

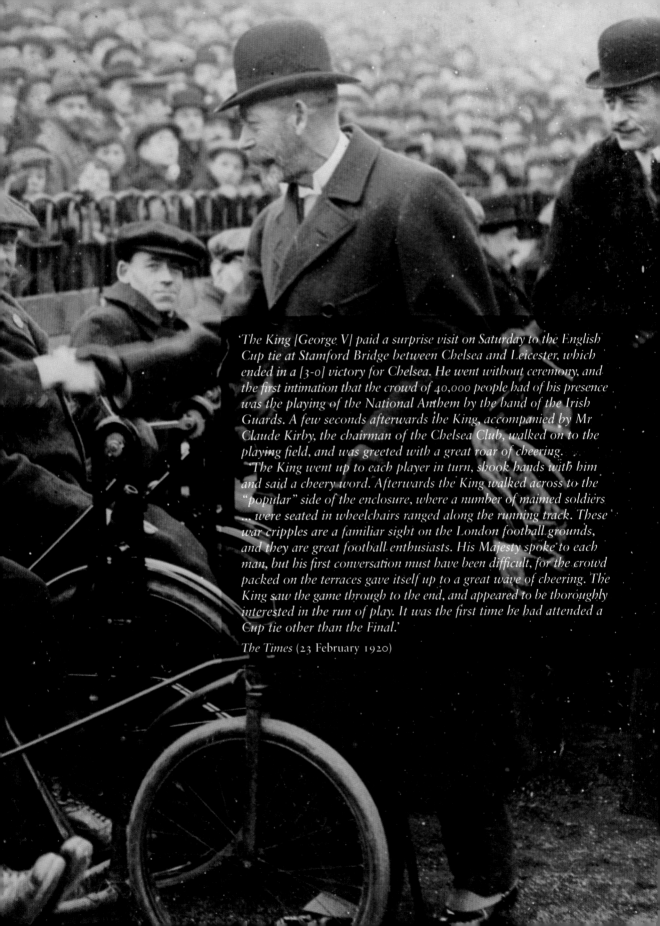

'The King [George V] paid a surprise visit on Saturday to the English Cup tie at Stamford Bridge between Chelsea and Leicester, which ended in a [3-0] victory for Chelsea. He went without ceremony, and the first intimation that the crowd of 40,000 people had of his presence was the playing of the National Anthem by the band of the Irish Guards. A few seconds afterwards the King, accompanied by Mr Claude Kirby, the chairman of the Chelsea Club, walked on to the playing field, and was greeted with a great roar of cheering.

The King went up to each player in turn, shook hands with him and said a cheery word. Afterwards the King walked across to the "popular" side of the enclosure, where a number of maimed soldiers ... were seated in wheelchairs ranged along the running track. These war cripples are a familiar sight on the London football grounds, and they are great football enthusiasts. His Majesty spoke to each man, but his first conversation must have been difficult, for the crowd packed on the terraces gave itself up to a great wave of cheering. The King saw the game through to the end, and appeared to be thoroughly interested in the run of play. It was the first time he had attended a Cup tie other than the Final.'

The Times (23 February 1920)

Even Spain's reigning monarch fancied the Blues. Alfonso XIII visited the Bridge in November 1919 to see Chelsea beat Bradford 4-0, a 'big performance [that] gave evident pleasure to the King of Spain, who watched the game all through and repeatedly applauded.'

Madrid added the prefix 'Real' after a similar visit a year later, the same time King George of England suddenly turned up at Stamford Bridge. Imagine the fuss today if Chelsea recieved such loyal support from royalty.

below With Crystal Palace unfit and Wembley not yet built, Frederick Parker's 1904 vision of the Bridge as a national stadium looked a possibility when the FA announced it would stage the 1920 FA Cup final. The match, in which Aston Villa beat Huddersfield Town 1-0 after extra time, was watched by 50,000 people. It meant valuable revenue for Chelsea, but not everyone was happy.

'The advantages of Stamford Bridge are limited to the stand running the length of the ground, and the huge terraces set out for the purpose of affording safety for the many thousands who must perforce stand throughout the game.

'On any Saturday the trouble in getting to see a league match need not be emphasised. It will not be attempted twice by any but the keenest followers of a particular team.

'Then after the game Fulham-road becomes impossible for vehicular traffic. To get away is more unpleasant than the agony of arriving. The narrow way behind the [East] stand means slow progress to the general crowd struggling to the street. The only safeguard against accidents every Saturday is the temperament of the British sportsmen. Ring seats on the cinder track round the playing pitch would enable some 80,000 people to see the game at Stamford Bridge and all those present would enjoy the match. But the sequel presents serious forebodings.' The Times (17 December 1919)

1921–1930

After the ups and downs of the 1910s, fans might have hoped the 1920s would offer more stability rather than more of the same. But it was business as usual: hiring the stars, building the image, attracting the crowds and failing to deliver consistency on the pitch. The club did win the London Challenge Cup, then a first-team tournament, by beating Clapton Orient 2-1 in November 1926, but that was it.

Stamford Bridge continued to be used as a neutral venue for big matches, including a couple more finals. The club was relegated under trying conditions in 1924 and only returned to the top league after an incredible three-month tour of South America in 1929. Mostly, though, there was shock at the activities of the Chelsea board: the club's new 'landlord' J.T. Mears, brother of founder Gus, was accused of overcharging scandalously for ground improvements and under-paying for his own refreshment licences. (The issue of his land ownership would echo through the years.) As Fred Parker had suspected it would, business was booming and amazement greeted the club's impressive financial figures, published in 1922.

In an article published on 29 July 1922 *Sports Pictures* revealed: 'The Chelsea Club, for a variety of reasons, is generally in the limelight, and once again they have set tongues wagging by the issue of a balance-sheet which carries us into the realms of high finance and show us a grand total on the revenue side of £75,075, or nearly £1,000 more than the gross income of Tottenham Hotspur. In comparing the two balance-sheets of these wealthy London clubs, I find that the gate receipts at

Chelsea were £70,568 and at Tottenham about £65,000, but whereas the actual profit made by the 'Spurs was £17,417, that of Chelsea was £11,796, which is partly accounted for by the fact that Tottenham are the freeholders of their ground, whereas Chelsea have to pay a pretty stiff rental.'

below Chelsea offered lots of 'added extras' to keep players sweet. Club president Lord Cadogan regularly opened his estate at Culford Hall for their recreation (as chairman Colonel Crisp did in Lewes a decade later) and mid-season breaks were the norm. In preparation for the FA Cup second round match at home to Southampton in early February 1923, the team enjoyed a break at Broadstairs in Kent. Here they are on the beach: (left to right) Tommy Meehan, Harry Ford, Bobby McNeil, Jack Harrow, John Priestley, Jimmy Armstrong, Steve Smith, Colin Hampton, Buchanan Sharp, David Cameron, Fred Linfoot, Harry Wilding, and long-serving trainer Jack Whitley.

'*Some great improvement has got to be recorded if they are to beat [lower league] Southampton. Still, I think, Chelsea will be able to rise to the occasion, and the change they have had at Broadstairs all the week should have toned them up and made them keen and eager.*' *Sports Pictures* (3 February 1923)

So much for rest cures. Chelsea drew 0-0 at the Bridge and lost the replay 0-1.

above In the mid-1920s magazines that covered sport, and particularly football, were immensely popular. Match previews and reports were often accompanied by humorous cartoons such as this one by George Chilmore for the match between Fulham and Chelsea at Craven Cottage in October 1924. The match ended 0-0, it was the fifth game in six that the Pensioners had failed to score.

Chelsea signings were still causing sensations. Tommy Meehan's arrival from Manchester United in 1920 was a coup, and he soon confirmed his status as one of the most skilful and stylish wing-halves of his era and 'quite the outstanding player on the Chelsea side.' His legend was assured for a time when his life was cut tragically short and 2,000 mourners attended his Wandsworth funeral, but the England international is wrongly overlooked now.

'At the end of 1920 he came to Chelsea among the stars, and there he twinkles with the best of them. They call Tommy a Terrier – some forwards have used stronger language. He's a full 90-minute man, on the go from whistle to whistle, and there's nothing he loves more than to see two big, hefty forwards standing opposite on the line-up. He worries 'em, he badgers 'em, confuses 'em, until their nerves and skill are torn to shreds – and then he worries them a bit more.' *Jack's Paper* (1922)

below Another star created in Walham Green was John 'Jack' Cock (pictured here having scored against Bolton Wanderers in 1920), a clever, tricky and stylish striker who thrived in west London, scoring 21 goals in 25 starts in his first season, 1919–20. The Cornishman with the matinee idol looks starred in football's first-ever feature film, *The Winning Goal*, in 1920, and two years later embarked on a part-time career in music hall which signalled the end of the love affair at the Bridge. Cock became a publican in south London after retiring from football.

'*Jack Cock was a great centre-forward for Chelsea. I remember him getting the ball in front of the opponents' goal, but with two defenders blocking any way through. So he feinted and turned a complete circle, causing one defender to turn right and the other left, both thinking he was going to pass the ball. But instead J.C. just created a gap and shot, for a brilliant goal.*'

John Marsh, supporter since 1921 (2006)

below Between the posts in the early 1920s was legendary amateur keeper Ben Howard Baker. A striking figure, at 6 foot 3 (seen here in action against West Brom in 1922) fans remember him 'bouncing the ball round his box, basketball style, while instructions were bellowed from the directors' box with a loudhailer'.

'*Ben Howard Baker was one of four goalkeepers who earned a cap by England while playing for Chelsea – he was a former record holder of the high jump. He was an amateur and the only goalkeeper to have scored for the club – even if it was a penalty. He was a popular figure but we were not always happy with him because he had a tendency to roam outside his area with unfortunate results. Together with [Jack] Harrow and [Jimmy] Sharp the trio formed a formidable defence.*'

John Marsh, supporter who saw his first Chelsea match in 1921 (2006)

right The void upfront of the misfiring Blues needed to be filled and inevitably the Pensioners' wallet came out again. After drawn-out speculation in the football press, Scotland international Andy Wilson signed from Middlesbrough (seen below in action against his old club), beginning a 50-year association with the club as player and supporter.

'The recent successes which have been achieved [by Chelsea] are largely due to Wilson. From his position of inside-left he is the real leader of the side, and though much of his work is done at a jog-trot, his passes are made with such a wonderful accuracy, and he has such a happy knack of picking out the man best placed to receive the ball that he ranks as one of the best constructive players in the game. His leisurely-going style, too, is deceptive. His very slowness is calculated to entice opponents into false positions. No man is better able to make effective use of the ball.' *The Times* (24 March 1927)

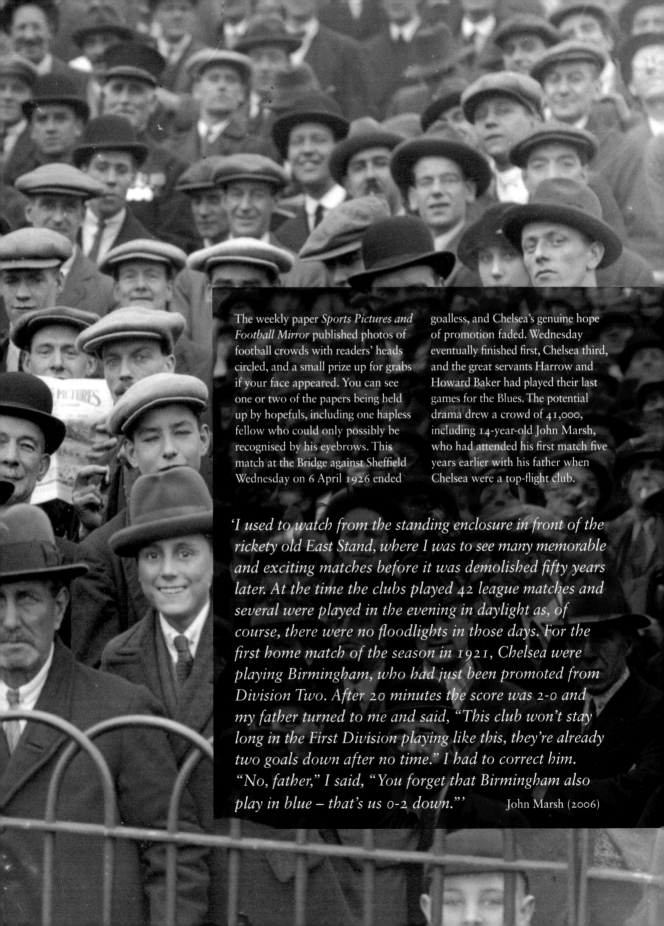

The weekly paper *Sports Pictures and Football Mirror* published photos of football crowds with readers' heads circled, and a small prize up for grabs if your face appeared. You can see one or two of the papers being held up by hopefuls, including one hapless fellow who could only possibly be recognised by his eyebrows. This match at the Bridge against Sheffield Wednesday on 6 April 1926 ended goalless, and Chelsea's genuine hope of promotion faded. Wednesday eventually finished first, Chelsea third, and the great servants Harrow and Howard Baker had played their last games for the Blues. The potential drama drew a crowd of 41,000, including 14-year-old John Marsh, who had attended his first match five years earlier with his father when Chelsea were a top-flight club.

'I used to watch from the standing enclosure in front of the rickety old East Stand, where I was to see many memorable and exciting matches before it was demolished fifty years later. At the time the clubs played 42 league matches and several were played in the evening in daylight as, of course, there were no floodlights in those days. For the first home match of the season in 1921, Chelsea were playing Birmingham, who had just been promoted from Division Two. After 20 minutes the score was 2-0 and my father turned to me and said, "This club won't stay long in the First Division playing like this, they're already two goals down after no time." I had to correct him. "No, father," I said, "You forget that Birmingham also play in blue – that's us 0-2 down."'

John Marsh (2006)

below Replacing Baker in goal for the Pensioners was Simeon, better known as 'Sam', Millington. Signed from non-league football in Shropshire, Millington became a hugely popular figure during his six years at Stamford Bridge. Here he repels an Arsenal attack in 1930.

'It's always the small details about the players that stand out and make you recall them. The first player I really took notice of was Sam Millington. He was a really reliable keeper and I remember he always wore a really large flat cap.'

Joe Cusselle, Chelsea Pensioner and supporter (2005)

below Bob Turnbull (second left) was the latest in a great line of Chelsea goalscorers, but even when he scored, as he did in the 2-3 FA Cup quarter-final defeat at Cardiff in March 1927, it was rarely enough with such a porous defence. Earlier in that campaign, however, Turnbull scored a hat-trick in the Blues' 7-2 away demolition of Accrington Stanley in front of 30,142, and top-scored with 23 in all competitions.

'*The Chelsea forwards finished almost as strongly as they had begun, and they must be given credit for a fine display of skill, speed and understanding. They were well-fed by their half-backs who were not so good in defence, where the outstanding figure was [Tommy] Law. Of the seven goals, three were obtained by Turnbull and two each by Wilson and [Albert] Thain. [Accrington's] real weakness lay in the total inability of the wing-half-backs to deal with the Chelsea outsides [Jackie Crawford and George Pearson], who outwitted them again and again with almost ludicrous ease.*'
The Times report of the Accrington Stanley match (31 January 1927)

'Frequently they would beat the top sides but lose to the lower ones. Often they would find themselves a goal or two down in the first half-hour and somebody would say, "Turn around and look at Joe's face." This was Chelsea vice-chairman Joseph [J.T.] Mears, sitting on the front row of the east stand. It would be a deep red, matching the colour of the carnation he used to have in his buttonhole.'

John Marsh (2003)

left Still the Pensioners were unpredictable, capable of raising or lowering their game according to the opposition. In March 1927, second tier Chelsea faced First Division strugglers Cardiff in the FA Cup quarter-finals at home and a remarkable attendance of more than 70,000 was recorded, with thousands more locked out (*below*), despite awful weather. As BBC radio reported, although Chelsea's half-backs – John Priestley, Harry Wilding and Willie Ferguson – enjoyed an afternoon of unfettered attacking, it was only full-backs Tommy Law, who 'got through the work of two men', and George Smith who kept the game goalless as the pitch became a quagmire.

Almost 50,000 watched the replay, a bad-tempered affair in which Chelsea never got going. Despite agonising near-misses late-on from Wilson and Bob Turnbull, Chelsea were out.

Chelsea's board found it hard to convince the players that a three month tour of South America was a cracking way to spend the summer break, but the ambitious idea worked. The itinerary (*below*) was gruelling. It started with a three-week journey on the steamship *Asturias* (*bottom*), during which the players relaxed and joined in the fun on deck with fellow passengers (*opposite left*). The schedule of 16 matches in Argentina, Uruguay (hosts of the first World Cup the following summer) and Brazil was forbidding, including two games on the same day 100 miles apart. The crowds and opposition players were often hostile, as the cartoon from the *Buenos Aires Herald* shows (*opposite bottom right*). It depicts the amazing game with a Buenos Aires XI at Boca Juniors stadium on 2 June, when all rules of football broke down. But over the six-week tour the party responded strongly and gelled together as a team, earning praise from the hosts – and promotion in May 1930.

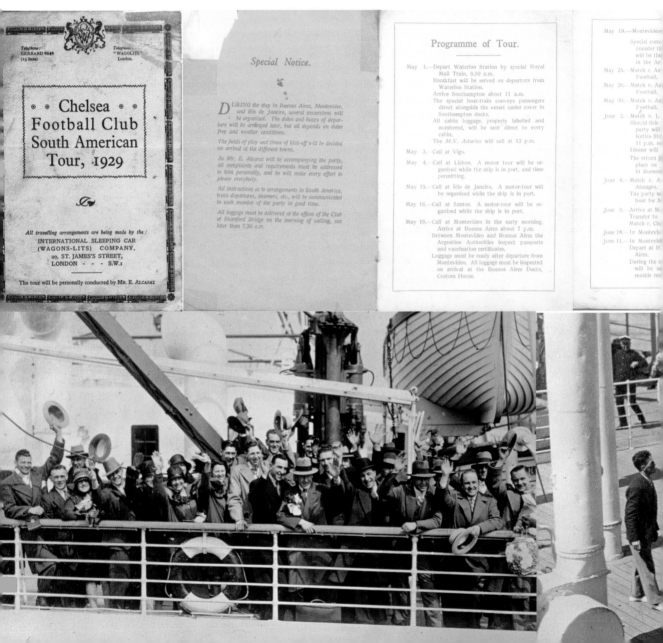

'When the Argentine captain kicked [George] Rodger in the groin, a happy shout went up. When Rodger fainted and was carried off the field, the public cheered in the same way their forefathers cheered when a Roman gladiator's bowels were ripped out on the arena. That Rodger had played the game he played every week of his life was no concern of theirs. I venture the hope that no more English teams will come here until the Argentine footballer has learnt to conduct himself like a sportsman.'

The *Buenos Aires Herald* report of the abandoned match at Boca Juniors stadium, Argentina (4 June 1929)

THEN CAPITAL SCORED AGAIN

CHELSEA PLAYERS THREW THEIR WEIGHT ABOUT AND

SPECTATORS THREW STONES ABOUT

The Brazilian leg of the tour provided Chelsea's first taste of samba football and Carioca fans, along with a first ever appearance under floodlights – against a combined Rio XI at Fluminense's sultry Rua Guanabara stadium.

below The style of play was as torrid as the weather. In the first match on 25 May against an all-star Buenos Aires XI at the barbed-wire fenced San Lorenzo de Almagro, Sam Millington acquitted himself brilliantly under pressure from

'Chelsea drew 1-1 after a brilliantly contested game. Can your readers picture a cloudless sky all day, with the thermometer at 90 degrees in the shade, then darkness at 6pm and this wonderful city illuminated with millions of lights. We were all entranced and our drive to the ground was full of interest. The home team were fine players, the goalkeeper performing excellently (all these South American custodians are as good as the very best in England) and their left-wing gave a splendid exhibition. The whole team, in fact, were speedy, controlled and trapped the ball magnificently, and took up positions admirably. Their fault was precisely that of our own side – the forwards dribbled and manoeuvred in front of goal until they were robbed. The crowd was most sportsmanlike, cheering us to the echo – quite a novel experience for us on this trip – and they let off rockets, squibs and detonators when the play pleased them. Everyone seemed pleased with the result.' Lt-Col Charles D. Crisp, Chelsea director (1929)

right The men who survived the Latin test in the summer went on to take the Second Division by storm, ushering in a new age of big names and huge crowds in the First.

Scopelli and Cherro with full back Tommy Law (left) looking on helplessly. Chelsea, 'los numerados', wearing numbered shirts for the first time and in a changed strip, triumphed 3-2. On 8 June (*below*)

Chelsea won 2-0 at the same stadium, with Fulham-born inside-right Albert Thain (pictured tracking back, along with Northern Ireland wing-half Sam Irving) grabbing one of the goals.

1931–1940

The 1930s were all about mass entertainment, glamour and novelty. Chelsea were foremost in bringing this to football. Stamford Bridge landlord and club director J.T. Mears, a leisure impresario who ran steamers up the Thames and a cinema in Kensington, introduced popular non-football ventures to Stamford Bridge. The board, soon to be decimated by the deaths of senior figures, underwrote more expensive forays into the transfer market by long-serving manager David Calderhead and his successor Leslie Knighton.

These included the greatest centre-forward of his day, Hughie Gallacher (pictured here teeing off with other players at Hoylake before the FA Cup match at Tranmere in 1932), as Chelsea's solid First Division status brought stability and record gates. In spite of the salary-cap, Chelsea was renowned as a comfortable, almost luxurious place to play your football with

little pressure to actually win anything – entertaining the crowd and reaching the odd semi-final always seemed to be good enough. But stability on the pitch was not always reflected off it, as legendary Nils Middelboe recalled in 1948:

'There are two kinds of director: the one who has a very good knowledge of football, and therefore adds positively to the club's sporting side; and the other who has a superficial knowledge of the game but still thinks he is an expert. The one who watches games from a special box, big cigar in mouth, wearing the club's colours in his buttonhole, and occasionally shouting towards the referees or players, often revealing how little he knows about football. He is something quite extraordinary – and is also the dangerous sort who can harm a club by interfering in the footballing side. Chelsea had quite a few of this type of director. When they were not at matches, they were very nice people to be around, sacrificing lots of time and money for the club; but unfortunately they didn't understand that they did more harm than good when they insisted on deciding the line-up of the team and the signing of new players.'

Hughie Gallacher, one of football's all-time greats, found it as easy to break Royal protocol as he did pre-match drink curfews. (He's pictured opposite at Highbury in 1932 touching the Prince of Wales while presenting the Chelsea team as skipper.) A restless genius, his arrival at Stamford Bridge from Newcastle for a rumoured new record fee of £12,000 in May 1930 crowned Chelsea's return to the top flight. At Chelsea – dubbed 'Little Caledonia'

– he teamed up with several Scots such as Alec Cheyne and Andy Wilson and two fellow 'Wembley Wizards' from the 1928 side that beat England: Tommy Law and Alec Jackson. His Stamford Bridge debut in September 1930, Chelsea's first Division One home match in six years, was a 6-2 win over Manchester United, watched by over 55,000, and set the right tone. A dapper, very modern striker, Hughie delighted crowds with his

brilliant shooting and trickery but had a troubled time at the club, where the West End nightlife and his hot temper meant trouble. A divorce settlement cost him a fortune he could not afford (the picture shows his wedding to second wife Hannah Anderson the same year, 1934) and after four and a half years the 'mighty atom' moved on, having netted a remarkable 81 goals in 144 appearances.

'The Chelsea forwards suggested that they would score goals against much stronger defences, particularly now they are settling down and getting to know each other's tricks. [Two-goal] Gallacher was dangerous whenever he got a foot to the ball and like Cheyne, who scored three goals, he was never afraid to shoot at goal. In the past there has been a marked disinclination on the part of the forwards to shoot, and goals have come as something of a surprise, but on Saturday every attack looked likely to end in a score, and double figures might have been reached.'

The Times' report of Gallacher's debut against Manchester United (8 September 1930)

'*[Sunderland's 18-year-old Alec Hastings] said, "I never hated anyone so much." From the kick-off Hughie snarled, baited and taunted the youngster throughout the game. But after the final whistle, Hughie went to the Sunderland dressing room and held out his hand, saying, "Good luck to you, son. You can take it. I'm sorry I needled you."*'

Paul Joannou, *The Hughie Gallacher Story* (1989)

'*Rising Sun, five to three? Come out mate, there's a match on!*'

1930s supporter Joe Smith remembers Gallacher (2006)

below Crowd favourite George Mills (*opposite*), caught in action against Leicester doing what he did best – scoring a goal – is one of Chelsea's great overlooked heroes. Signed first as an amateur and styled G.R. Mills, he turned pro and scored 123 goals in 239 official games between 1929 and 1939. That despite often being the first to make way for a new forward – and at Chelsea there were always new forwards. Reminiscent of latter-day hero Ian Hutchinson in his fearless style of play, Mills saw off big names such as Gallacher, Cheyne and Bambrick and became an England international. His chief distinction, though, is that on 13 November 1937, his goal in the 1-4 defeat at Everton made Mills the first Chelsea player to hit a century of league goals. 'Gatling Gun' Hilsdon's range fell just short on 98, and although hot-shot Bob Thomson managed a ton during First World War football, those games were 'unofficial'. Only five players in Chelsea's history have surpassed Mills's total in all competitions: Bobby Tambling (202), Kerry Dixon (193), Roy Bentley and Peter Osgood (both 150) and Jimmy Greaves (132).

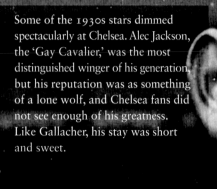

Some of the 1930s stars dimmed
spectacularly at Chelsea. Alec Jackson,
the 'Gay Cavalier,' was the most
distinguished winger of his generation,
but his reputation was as something
of a lone wolf, and Chelsea fans did
not see enough of his greatness.
Like Gallacher, his stay was short
and sweet.

'A big star will sometimes put up the "gate" by six or seven thousand,
and there was no doubt that Jackson appealed to the public. For a
time, he did magnificently. Then came trouble. This was all before
my time at Stamford Bridge, and I only know the rumours of the
disturbance that spread like wildfire through the football world
when Jackson was dropped from the first team. After a long talk I
came to the view, rightly or wrongly, that he could not recover the
speed and stamina required for big football, no matter how hard he
might work, for he was no longer a youth. So that, no matter how
I – and the fans – hated it, there was nothing else for Chelsea to do
than to put their £9,000 star on the transfer list at £4,000. Even that
was useless. No big club signed him up. A great winger – but he would
not fit into every team. With a different temperament he might have
won to greater heights even than he did.'

Leslie Knighton, Chelsea manager 1933–39 (1948)

'In World War Two Woodley continued to play for Chelsea though not for England – as a small boy, I used to watch him and wonder how anyone could beat him – while Jackson was lent to their London rivals, Brentford. When the clubs met, though it was only in the ersatz wartime, "unofficial," football, Chelsea wouldn't let Jackson play against them!'   Brian Glanville (2005)

left Young Vic Woodley (here tipping over athletically against Sunderland in November 1937) was a brilliant keeper for Chelsea and England, but an early injury and concern over his lack of experience had meant the club still went up and bought his equally highly-rated Scotland counterpart Johnny Jackson from Partick Thistle in 1933. The two never opposed each other internationally, nor in the Chelsea camp, despite the period 1936–38 during which the usually infallible Woodley could let in four goals and still keep his place. The situation has its echo in the positions of goalkeepers Petr Cech and Carlo Cudicini in the 21st century.

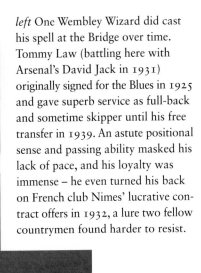

left One Wembley Wizard did cast his spell at the Bridge over time. Tommy Law (battling here with Arsenal's David Jack in 1931) originally signed for the Blues in 1925 and gave superb service as full-back and sometime skipper until his free transfer in 1939. An astute positional sense and passing ability masked his lack of pace, and his loyalty was immense – he even turned his back on French club Nimes' lucrative contract offers in 1932, a lure two fellow countrymen found harder to resist.

When J.T. Mears bought the freehold to Stamford Bridge from late brother Gus's estate in spring 1921, he became Chelsea's landlord, leasing the ground to the club from September to April, while keeping the summer months to himself for other money-spinning activities. Although the baseball and athletics meetings that controversially damaged the playing surface eventually departed the grounds, in May 1928 the running track was converted to launch Australian speedway, then known as 'dirt track' (the picture opposite shows riders W. Banner and F. Cooper at the Bridge in 1930). In its first two seasons the promoter is said to have made as much as £40,000 profit, of which Mears took a handsome cut. Dirt track was replaced in 1932 by the even more lucrative greyhound racing. The first Chelsea heard about it was a request from the Greyhound Racing Association for an agreement to run races during the football season for £5,000 a year. While the south terrace development (known later, partially roofed, as the Shed) had begun in 1930, the new greyhound company embarked on stadium developments solely for the benefit of its bookmakers and punters, including the kennels, Tote booths and Totalisator board that tracked betting (*below*). The dogs were a controversial but popular feature at the stadium until the hare was retired on 13 July 1968.

'*By the turnstiles were the price boards. After the football, they'd take out the football admission price cards and the prices went up for the dogs. Punters used to run round to the halfway line to look across to see who won the race, then run back and have another bet. Anybody who wanted to throw out the dogs was barmy. It's a wonderful income, produces a lot of money, gambling; never mind if it takes up another six yards of the pitch.*'

Joe Smith, Stamford Bridge street vendor (2006)

This image, surely one of the great portrayals of a football match, was painted by local artist Charles Cundall, RA. He perched on a wooden platform at the back of the north end of Stamford Bridge for the visit of Arsenal among 82,905 fans – the second biggest English league attendance ever. The game finished 1-1, Bambrick scoring Chelsea's opener after good work by Mitchell and Argue.

below Though the legendary inconsistency ruled out honours, Chelsea played some brilliant stuff and became one of the biggest draws in 1930s football. Scots inside-forward George Gibson provided a magical moment, scoring against Sunderland at the Bridge before 65,000 people in September 1935.

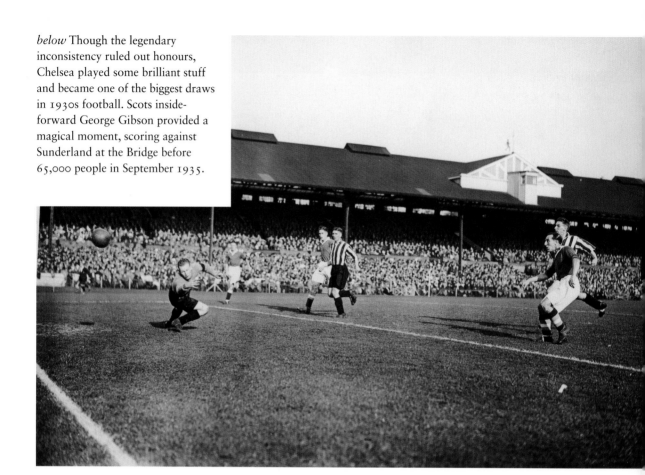

'*Gibson, picking up a pass somewhere near the halfway line, scored a magnificent and completely unexpected goal. There seemed no danger to Sunderland for at least three of their players were within tackling distance, but Gibson evaded a tackle and, by a combination of body swerve and deception, went through the defence as though he were invisible and, on arriving in the goalmouth, had time both to look round and to pick the precise spot in the net where he meant to place the ball.*'   The Times (30 September 1935)

above 'Notice must surely be taken of Chelsea' gushed one reporter after the opening day of the 1937–38 season and a 6-1 drubbing for Liverpool. George Mills scored a hat-trick alongside big guns Burgess, Mitchell and Argue. On 23 October, euphoria on the Fulham Road: goals from Bambrick and Argue against Brentford put the Blues top for the first time in many, many years. It didn't last, and a tenth-place finish was scant return from a star-studded squad.

As with other clubs, Chelsea found continental touring therapeutic – for the finances as well as morale – and the 1930s brought some great jollies for directors and players, as Johnny Jackson's itinerary for the 1937 tour of the Balkans, Austria, Italy and France reveals (*below*). A year earlier, as Adolf Hitler planned world domination, the club took in Sweden, Holland and Poland (programme

for the match v Wisla Krakow, *opposite bottom right*), and, quaintly, stopped off in Nazi-run Berlin for breakfast on the way back.

In the 1940s and 1950s the touring parties included directors' wives, but as they set out from Liverpool docks in May 1935 (*bottom*) for the brief jaunt to a benefit match at Linfield, Belfast, those accompanying the team were

long-serving trainer Jack Whitley (back, wearing a Homburg), manager Leslie Knighton (middle, smoking a cigarette) and veteran chairman Claude Kirby (the grey-haired gent next to him). The players often each received substantial tour mementos, such as this goblet presented to Billy Mitchell by AIK from Stockholm in Sweden in 1936.

'The tours they went on were magnificent. They were like holidays for the directors. Footballers were some of the few people in the country with passports. My father's was personally signed by the Foreign Secretary. They'd be away for a month or so – virtually every country in Europe, my father's been. I've got the itineraries: all the players who went and the staff. When they stopped off in Berlin Hitler was in power. There was massive reconstruction going on, roads being built everywhere, to every border. He said the worst place they went to was Poland. My father always said he was shot at from the side of the pitch because he'd shoulder-charged one of the Polish players. After that Dickie Spence said to him, "Don't come near me – they're shooting at you!"'

Martin, son of Chelsea player Harry Burgess (2005)

Amid the relative stability on the pitch, there were some major shocks off it. David Calderhead was released in June 1933 with a gold medal for long service after 24 fruitless years as secretary-manager. He was succeeded by Leslie Knighton, photographed here (*below*) on his first day, sharing a tab on the terraces with chairman Claude Kirby. Kirby, chairman since the club was founded, was one of four senior figures to die suddenly within six months of each other. The passing of Bert Palmer, assistant secretary since 1905, then vice-chairman and landowner J.T. Mears (September 1935), Kirby (October the same year) and his successor Charles Pratt (February 1936) robbed the club of priceless experience at a time of major rebuilding. Although Lt-Col C.D. Crisp (late of Arsenal) steadied the ship as chair, J.T.'s son Joe Mears would emerge as the club's dominant force for the next 30 years. As early as November 1933 young Joe had vetoed a board decision to give the manager complete jurisdiction over team selection, and in January 1937 he insisted that 'the teams be chosen by the manager with the co-operation of the directors' – a decision Knighton had to ride with until his replacement by Billy Birrell in May 1939.

Leslie Knighton specialised in crossing the Irish Sea to bring the best from the north of Ireland, partitioned from the south a decade earlier. The new players had varying impacts at the Bridge: Tom Priestley, a fledgling 'football genius' who cost the earth, left mysteriously after one season; Joe Bambrick (*opposite*) had scored a double hat-trick for Ireland against Wales in 1930, joined Chelsea in 1934 aged 29 and wowed the crowd for four seasons.

above Billy Mitchell, another Irish import, was a popular and wholehearted player over many seasons. He is seen here (centre) playing against Leicester City in September 1938. Chelsea won 3-0.

'Mitchell and Bambrick [were] two universally loved Irish internationals. Joe Bambrick was, I believe, the most popular man locally who ever stepped out of Irish football. His skilful play, his geniality and his first-class sportsmanship on the field so endeared him to the hearts of those in his own country that he was for many years their chief sports idol. We got [Mitchell] at a most reasonable figure and I do not exaggerate when I say that within a single season Chelsea would not have taken twenty times what they paid for him.' Manager Leslie Knighton (1948)

'One day I threw such a particularly long ball that the distance was measured and found to be 48 yards.'

Sam Weaver, explaining his art in a BBC radio profile of Chelsea FC (11 February 1939)

A boy beats the slouches heading for the Bridge in a busy matchday scene outside the old Chelsea & Fulham railway station on Wandon Road. In a few years, thousands of soldiers from Dunkirk disembarked here and were met with cups of tea by locals.

'There were some cottages opposite the station – they must be worth a fortune now. And a lady in one of them used to take in bikes at six-pence a go. Joe Payne used to leave his there. I can see Joe now: rotten old bike, ruffled hair, taking his clips off to go and play for Chelsea.'

Joe Smith (2006)

below Billy Birrell was Chelsea's third Scots manager but the first to ditch the 'secretary' part of the title, which was taken on by Harry Palmer. Birrell, rarely seen without his pipe and trilby, objected to the escalating price of players, but his ambitious plans for youth development were stalled by the war. He's pictured here with newly appointed trainer Arthur Stollery, a South African soon replaced by Norman Smith. Smith introduced new fitness methods to the former regime of Jack Whitley. In 1947, as Notts County manager, Stollery splashed a British record £20,000 Chelsea's way to take away Tommy Lawton, who'd fallen out with the board.

below In August 1939–40, the Football League finally sanctioned full use of numbered shirts for the first time. Among those running out for this pre-season public trial are Mills (9), Salmond (5) and Mitchell (4). Under innovative chairman Claude Kirby, Chelsea had first worn numbered shirts on 25 August 1928 against Swansea, and then at the start of their three-month tour of South America in 1929 they became known as 'los numerados'.

1941–1950

Once again a decade was riven by conflict, but this time the Luftwaffe's bombing brought the war far closer to home. Football was again regionalised and de-professionalised. Footballers joined the armed forces or essential services. And, as if the novelty of a different diet increased the appetite, Chelsea again thrived, winning silverware and enjoying star guests who would become household names. Incredibly, three future England managers wore the royal blue.

But when war ended and the professional game was restored, Chelsea suffered like everyone else the anxieties of peace. Like the rest of war-torn London, the club's first task was rebuilding. The pre-war squad was almost as shattered as the capital's docks, the stadium was creaking. So while manager Billy Birrell launched the club's first

proper youth scheme, Chelsea, as usual, splashed out on the star forwards of the day, and one of British football's biggest ever matches was staged at Stamford Bridge – the visit of Moscow Dynamo. For young Fulham schoolboy Roy Simpson, getting in to see the game was of the utmost importance: 'It was something different. It was a new team, from Russia. They'd given the Nazis hell in beating them back. Partly we were curious at what the Russians were like, but also we wanted to see what sort of football they played. See if it was at all different football. So when they come over, people were well interested, wanted to see them. They climbed up over the Shed on to the roofs. It was something brand new for them to see. Everybody was talking about it – "Why not go? Let's go." We were all bunking off school to go and see the Dynamos. That's why you get the 100,000 at Chelsea.'

When Chelsea had lost 1-4 to Bologna, in the final of the Paris Exhibition tournament in 1937, the Italian coach had declared it a great day for Fascism. A mood of war prevailed and in 1938–39 many footballers had joined others enlisting for national service work in their leisure time (*right*, two players arriving at the Bridge in uniform). As hostilities began 23-year-old Scouser Harry Cothliff was Chelsea's first 'casualty' – his proposed £6,000 move from Torquay to Stamford Bridge died the day war broke out. Blackouts were enforced, travel restricted, crowds were limited by decree. Regional Football Leagues were re-established, and once again guest players provided brief excitement. Unlike in 1914–18, though, the game was regarded as good for morale, and a uniform guaranteed reduced entry fees to the terraces (*opposite left*). Soon the battle-weary could be seen on the terraces (*opposite right*).

'What would have happened if the Spotter had seen a bomber overhead?'
'We'd have directed it over Highbury!'

Conversation at a Stamford Bridge reminiscence session (1990s)

'AIR RAID WARNING. *In the event of an Air Raid Warning the ground exits will be opened, so that those who wish to leave can do so. Play will proceed unless the "Spotter" reports enemy activity in the vicinity.'* Chelsea Chronicle (1941)

'Whereabouts of Players who were on the Club's books at the beginning of the season may be of interest: The following joined the Police War Reserve some twelve months ago and were called up just prior to the commencement of hostilities: Alexander, Barber, Buchanan, Burgess, Foss, Griffiths, Hanson, Jackson, Mills, O'Hare, Payne, Salmond, Sherborne, Smale, Smith A. J., Spence, Tennant, Vaux, Weaver and Woodley. Bidewell and Mayes are serving in His Majesty's Fighting Forces, and of the remainder: Argue, White, Kilpatrick, McMillan and Creighton have returned to Scotland, Mitchell has joined his family in Ireland, James is at his home in Wales, and Smith, our recruit from Port Vale, has returned to the Midlands, and will assist his former club until he attains military age and receives his call to the Colours.'

Chelsea Chronicle (30 September 1939)

below Some of the servicemen-footballers who made a temporary home at Chelsea were very distinguished. This photo shows Joe Mercer, Frank Swift, Tommy Walker and Tommy Lawton in their military attire. Mercer, along with Walter Winterbottom, Matt Busby, Billy Liddell, Charlie Mitten, George Hardwick, George Swindin, Reg Mountford, Eddie Hapgood, Frank Soo and others, all graced the Bridge at various stages between 1939 and 1946. Winterbottom and Mercer, like wartime Chelsea team-mate Ron Greenwood, went on to manage England. Fellow guests Johnny Harris, Danny Winter and Len Goulden joined Walker and Lawton in signing for the Pensioners when the war was over.

above Even in Chelsea's illustrious history of forwards, few had arrived with a claim to fame as impressive as that of Joe Payne, pictured on the prowl in his debut against Bolton. In 1936, he'd scored all but two of Luton's 12 goals against Bristol Rovers, and was universally known as 'Ten-Goal'. He moved to Stamford Bridge in 1938 for an eventful time even before the advent of war. The day he nabbed his first hat-trick, for example, against Middlesbrough in early 1939, he had previously been knocked out cold by a team-mate's shot. But poacher Payne's greatest arena was the unofficial wartime Football League South. In 1939–40 he hit the target an impressive 34 times, but in 1943–44 he knocked in an amazing 50 goals in 35 games, and 40 in 28 the following campaign.

Two-footed and with a powerful header, Payne could score from anywhere. He moved to West Ham United in 1946.

Chelsea had been defeated 1-3 by Charlton in the Football League South Cup final the previous year, so it was a pleasure to return to a packed Wembley Stadium in April 1945 with a more favourable outcome – even if it took a couple of non-Blues to get the goals. Incidentally, so great was interest in the match that the Football League returned £30,000 worth of ticket applications.

FOOTBALL WAR CUP

PRESENTED by W. J. CEARNS, ESQ

'The King and Queen and Princess Elizabeth were present at Wembley when Chelsea won the League South Cup by beating Millwall by two goals to none. Before the match the teams were presented to the King, who afterwards handed the cup to Harris, Chelsea's captain. The crowd of 90,000 must have been sadly disappointed at the quality of the play, for neither side was ever able to get into its stride. If one of them deserved a cup it was Chelsea. For ten minutes after the interval Chelsea, who had moved Wardle inside and put Smith at outside-right, showed something approaching their normal form. Within two minutes Goulden ... nodded the ball to McDonald, who took it on the volley and gave Bartram no chance. Five minutes later a shot from Payne struck a defender and Wardle [of Exeter City]... kept his head and scored the second goal from short range.'

The Times (9 April 1945)

below right The team that won the 1945 League South Cup final. Left to right, back: J. Shaw, assistant manager, George Wardle (Exeter City), Joe Payne, Ian Black (Aberdeen), George Hardwick (Middlesbrough), Jack McDonald (Bournemouth), Norman Smith (trainer), Charlie Freeman (assistant trainer); front: Bobby Russell, Les Smith (Brentford), Johnny Harris (Wolves, captain), Billy Birrell (manager-secretary), Danny Winter (Bolton), Len Goulden (West Ham United), Dickie Foss.

'I was there to watch Dad. He thought it was an awful game, but Chelsea won 2-0. Chelsea played in red and Millwall played in their blue strip. (One of the players stood out on the Millwall side. He had very bright ginger hair.) There were 90,000 people there. That's not bad, is it, for just as the war was ending?'

Roy, son of Len Goulden (2006)

'The above Lads, with two exceptions, have carried the brunt of the season's campaigning, and while comparisons are always odious, one may be permitted to say that the half-back line has proved to be the backbone of our success. Bobby Russell, Johnny Harris and Dicky Foss together have played with such solidity and resource that the team was permitted to weather most storms on a level keel. In the rear, Ian Black with Danny Winter and George Hardwick had so much in hand that only four goals were conceded in twice as many Cup games. Up in front a much-changed attack contrived to score, in all, one hundred and eleven goals. Joe Payne has helped himself to forty of those and had much to do with a successful attack.'

Chelsea Chronicle (21 April 1945)

In peacetime it didn't take long for Chelsea to flex its financial muscle in an attempt to draw the crowds back to Stamford Bridge. Four of the biggest acquisitions were England's greatest centre-forward Tommy Lawton from Everton for £14,000 (*below*, firing in a typically powerful header towards the Birmingham goal on his debut at the Bridge in November 1945 in front of 53,000 – the biggest attendance there in six years); Scotland's 'ace of Hearts', inside-forward Tommy Walker (*below right*, signing autographs at his last match at the Bridge in 1948); West Ham and England's Len Goulden, and Johnny Harris (*opposite*, with Walker, left, and Goulden, top, in 1945). With Harris as skipper and a new, stellar forward line, Chelsea became the biggest attraction in London.

'Tommy [Lawton] was the man, God bless his soul. Can England have him back please? He'd show them where to put the ball. Just before he died he came to Stamford Bridge and popped by my stall, and nobody knew who he was. I said to people, "Excuse me, this is England's greatest centre-forward!"'

Joe Smith, Stamford Bridge stallholder (2006)

'Tommy Walker – marvellous player! What a player! Tall and lean. He was brave, used to get in with his head, and was a wonderful passer of the ball, lovely 30-yard balls and great to watch. But because he was lean he got knocked off the ball quite a lot.'

Roy Simpson, supporter (2005)

'I don't think they talked about the game, just went out and played, enjoyed themselves, acted on their own natural instincts and how to play with each other. I'm sure there wasn't too much tactics. They knew they were playing against good players but they didn't go out and try to deal with those players in a technical sense like they do today. Lawton was a tremendous target man. Dad was up and down, up and down. Tommy Walker was very quiet, very nice man.'

Roy, son of Len Goulden, who attended every home game (2006)

Such was the interest in the visit of Russia's Moscow Dynamo in November 1945 that tens of thousands broke down the gates, lining the pitch and scaling any structure in and around the ground (*opposite*). Estimates as to the attendance range between 80,000 and 100,000 people. Such damage was done to surrounding buildings by the unstoppable hordes that it was technically deemed a riot. The sensational game finished in a diplomatic 3-3 draw and was talked about for years.

'The Russians do not dribble. They flash the ball from man to man in bewildering fashion, often while standing still. Only when there is a clear run to goal does the Dynamo really whirl into action. Then seven men converge like destroyers on the opposing goal.'

Tommy Lawton (1946)

above A bunch of posies... Moscow Dynamo say it with flowers to hand to their opponents before the match.

right Reg Williams tackles the flying Stankevich – the ball rebounds into the net to put Chelsea 2-0 up.

'I should have been at school but I can remember sitting up there in the east stand watching everybody clambering up through the girders. The commentary box was in a gantry right at the front of the stand and there were people climbing up that and getting onto the actual stand roof. I saw at least one person come through the roof of the stand. The crowd was actually on the touchline. Don't forget there was a dog track there, which was covered as well; they obviously led people there to avoid any tragedies happening. When [before the kick-off] the Russians handed over a posy to each Chelsea player, Dad was shocked and I think they all were. It's a Russian tradition, so fair enough – it certainly wasn't a British tradition! The Dynamo players looked different, they played different.'   Roy, son of Len Goulden (2006)

In summer 1946 a chance to toughen himself up at Stamford Bridge for a film role as young gangster Pinkie Brown in *Brighton Rock* started a lifelong love affair between actor and director Richard, now Lord Attenborough, and Chelsea FC. He trained with the players and in return invited them onto the set at Welwyn Studios, (*above*) where Tommy Lawton and the squad, plus Joe Mears, met his co-star Carol Marsh (seated). He became a Chelsea director for 15 years and is life Vice-President of the club.

right Members of the supporters' club on an outing to Wolves.

'*Chelsea were not exactly high society, but they had a lot of showbiz supporters, being off the West End and the King's Road. It's not like the players paraded down there, but people like Richard Attenborough were there and would bring famous people round.*'

Roy, son of Len Goulden (2006)

above Richard Attenborough larking around with Tommy Lawton and Albert Tennant.

'One of the things the director said to me was, "Dick, we've got to slim you down. So, number one, you go on a diet. Number two, we have to get you fit so that you're lithe etc. – do you follow a football team?" So I said no, not particularly. My father-in-law, Sheila's dad, had taken us in 1941, '42, '43 to both Chelsea and Fulham, so I sort of plumped for Chelsea, not particularly with any huge passion. [Director] John Boulting rang [then Chelsea manager] Billy Birrell and said could this young actor come and do some training to get himself fit with the team? One of the papers, Picture Post or someone, came and covered it. So there was Tommy Lawton, Albert Tennant, Tommy Walker, Len Goulden, Dickie Spence, Johnny Harris etc. I've got a number of pictures, like this, of me, ostensibly, being given "the works" by the boys. The result was that I became a huge fan of Chelsea and my pal became Tommy [Lawton]. Tommy was on £18 a week, and I think £1/10s or £2 if they won, and £1 if they drew. Tom, because he knew I'd got bugger all money, in the same way that he didn't either, would always leave me two tickets at the Players' Entrance. I had an old Jaguar at that time, and Poppy [his wife] and I used to go to all the away games 1947, '48, '49.'

Richard, Lord Attenborough (2006)

In 1947 Billy Birrell condemned the high cost of transfers and instigated a far-sighted youth development programme that would have a hugely positive effect on Chelsea's squads down the years. Under the name Tudor Rose, and coached by former players Dickie Foss (*below and opposite left*) and Albert Tennant (*opposite bottom right*), along with Len Goulden (*opposite top right*), the juniors were put through their paces. They played Saturday matches at the Welsh Harp ground, off the North Circular Road near Hendon and trained the following day.

'This "Chelsea scheme" is different from the numerous other junior football schemes. For it sets out to make youngsters not only good footballers but first-rate citizens. Infinite trouble is taken in giving everyone a thorough chance and Chelsea's reward is a constant flow of young players from their Junior club into their various senior teams.'

John Graydon, *The FA Book For Boys* (1949)

'There were a lot of boys wanting to improve themselves and they got in touch with Chelsea and Dad took training every Sunday morning on the Stamford Bridge pitch and I would go with him. The Welsh Harp wasn't the best of places, especially when the wind blew off that lake. It was pretty bleak. There were a few good players later when I faced them in the 1950s. They seemed to favour big strong lads. Cliff Huxford was a big bloke, Tony Nicholas, big blond boy, Barry Sluman, strong stocky player, Roy Fergie, I think was a full-back, Johnny Compton who went to Ipswich. Roy Cunningham, big centre-half. Davy Court. Yeah, they had a very good side. Ronnie Tindall was there, very nice player. David Cliss used to say that when they played Arsenal, Dickie would feed them oxblood pills – that's what they said. And Dickie used to say to Cliff Huxford, "Kick him up the arse – I want him to feel it." I played for Arsenal Youth against Chelsea, who always had a very good side, and I got caught once or twice, and it hurt!'

Roy Goulden, son of Len and former Arsenal junior (2006)

1951–1960

While Billy Birrell's progress had been stunted by war, Ted Drake's arrival as manager in 1952 sparked a revolution at Chelsea Football Club from top to bottom. A first casualty was the old Pensioner emblem, unrepresentative of Drake's new model 'Blues'.

The young Chelsea boss, supported on the field by his great skipper and striker Roy Bentley (centre, netting the winner against Sheffield United in November 1955) and in the boardroom by chairman Joe Mears, built a great

team mostly of graft more than glamour. He also threw more resources at the youth scheme – the first major graduates of which were starting to have an impact – and even demanded more biased vocal support from Chelsea's traditionally sporting fans: 'I want more people to live, sleep and breathe Chelsea Football Club,' he said. In the groundbreaking age of jet planes, cool jazz and TV, relegation was avoided by the barest of margins, the title was won at last and old music hall jibes put to bed, albeit temporarily. And if the novel European Cup adventure had to be overlooked, continental teams still lit up Stamford Bridge.

Skipper Roy Bentley acknowledged the effect of Drake's arrival as the club celebrated back-to-back Premiership victories in 2006: 'What Ted gave us was heart, a great family feeling. Nobody felt excluded. Ted introduced ballwork in training, something almost unheard of at most clubs. And there was so much competition for places. Nobody could afford to relax. We used to be a vaudeville joke. Ted changed that. He even changed the club motif and replaced the Chelsea Pensioner with a lion.'

It wasn't all glamour in the early
1950s. The team strips were
transported in kit skips, like this
one outside the team coach
attended by Johnny Harris. Note
the smart new blazer badges,
eventually to make way for the
famous rampant lion.

No pictorial history should be
without the ritual team bath shot.
This one, taken at Stamford Bridge
in the early 1950s, features key men
Stan Willemse, Ken Armstrong,
Johnny Harris and Roy Bentley
among others, but not a single bar
of soap.

Statistics, eh? In the 1950–51 season Billy Birrell's team maintained top-flight status by the microscopic margin of 0.044 on goal average (goals for, divided by goals against). After 14 matches without tasting victory, wins against Liverpool, Wolves (the picture below shows Ken Armstrong's disputed winner in the 2–1 victory) and Fulham made sure it all went down to the final weekend, with the Pensioners hosting lacklustre Bolton Wanderers and the other candidates for the drop, Everton and Sheffield Wednesday, facing each other. Roy Bentley and teenager Bobby Smith shared the spoils in a surprisingly emphatic 4-0 win.

'Staying up at that Bolton game was unreal – for us to stay up we had to win by a minimum of three goals, and Sheffield Wednesday had to beat Everton by five goals too. Then amazingly, by half-time we're 3-0 up. And then on the electric scoreboard it said that Wednesday were winning 4-0 – the roar in the ground when that went up was absolutely amazing. In those days radio commentaries never went on till the second half, and Wednesday was the commentary game, so you had people getting more and more excited, "It's five now!" Wednesday won 6-0 and we won 4-0, and everybody was trying to do the maths to work out the goal averages. In the end we stayed up by 0.044 and Everton and Wednesday went down.'

Chris Gibbons, Stamford Bridge tour guide (2006)

below After the trauma of 1950–51, Johnny Harris and Roy Bentley found themselves in dispute with Chelsea over pay levels and the quality of the squad. They held out for eight weeks without a salary until 25 August. Both were tormented by the row. Harris sneaked onto the terraces among fans in disguise. Bentley 'walked along the Thames embankment, near to tears over Chelsea.' Thankfully the issues were settled and both returned, with satisfactory results all round. The picture of pro-Bentley graffito on the main gates shows the strength of public feeling when things turned sour again in the summer of 1956. Bentley was left out of the side and soon opted for a move to Fulham, his first appearance there putting 5,000 on the gate.

opposite top Frank Blunstone (left, in action against West Bromwich Albion) has often been called the baby of the title-winning team – he was 20 when the season closed – but it could be said he was also the heartbeat. He was old enough to do national service in the medical corps in 1954–55, a season in which, from his base at Aldershot, he played four times a week for Chelsea, the army, and England. And he was spirited enough to drive the team forward again and again with his pacy flank play.

Loved by the fans, when injury ended 'head-down Frankie's' career in the early 1960s he was allowed to set up Chelsea's first official club shop and, as a youth team coach, he helped nurture the likes of Alan Hudson and Ray Wilkins.

'Ted always reckoned his best-value signings for Chelsea were Frank Blunstone, £7,000 from Crewe, and Peter Sillett, £12,000 from Southampton. In February 1953, to sign Frank, an England left-winger-to-be who was only 18, Ted drove up to Crewe Alexandra and took their board meeting by surprise with an offer they just couldn't refuse.'
Albert Sewell, Chelsea programme editor (2005)

below Bobby Smith was a powerful target man and perhaps the first brilliant product of Birrell's three-year-old youth scheme. He made his debut in 1950 and scored 30 times in 86 games, including this goal, part of a great hat-trick in the cup against Leeds in 1952, before being snapped up in 1955 by Billy Nicholson of Tottenham.

Bustling former Arsenal and England striker Ted Drake may not have been the board's first choice as manager Billy Birrell's replacement in 1952, but his recent success at Reading convinced them that he was a chance worth taking. They were proved right. These pictures show key figures in his regime: shrewd skipper Bentley, winger Eric Parsons and elegant wing-half Ken Armstrong jogging along Fulham Road in July 1953 (*far left*); and trainer Jack Oxberry and scout Tom Robinson, with Drake, (*left*), watching the team in pre-season the same year. Drake predicted he would make Chelsea competitive in three years and he was as good as his word, delivering the title in 1955 with a single-mindedness and energy that no previous Chelsea boss could manage.

In 1953 the Football Association created a competition for artists. One thousand seven hundred football-related works of art were entered for the £1,000 prize, including many with Chelsea as a subject. This painting is local artist Chris Chamberlain's view of Chelsea versus Arsenal on Good Friday that year, described by one critic as 'among the more ambitious works … an animated scene'. Chamberlain's brush really captured the colourful atmosphere of the 1950s: the magnetism of the old stadium and its ornate gates, the blue and red crowd filing along Fulham Road and in from side streets, a policeman on horseback, the favour sellers, and the Rising Sun, scene of many a last-minute gulp of ale before entering the ground. A copy of this painting hangs in the Millennium foyer of

the West Stand. The FA's prize was eventually split four ways. Laurence Toynbee, whose wonderful football scenes at the Bridge still hang at Langan's Brasserie in London (*see page 178*), received £250 for his efforts.

'*I've said this for years: if you had crocodiles in the Fulham Road and Chelsea was at home to Biggleswade, they would still cross the crocodiles to get in and watch them.*'

Badge vendor Joe Smith (2006)

below Johnny McNichol, Ted Drake's first signing in August 1952, was another of the championship-winning side's heroes. This curler, one of two goals against Charlton in August 1953, was among the 18 scored by the forward that helped Chelsea up to eighth in the First Division, the club's highest finish in almost 20 years.

'McNichol was a very underrated player, a skilful and stylish inside forward. He lacked pace and was not what you'd call a striker, but he was a creator, an attacking midfielder like Lampard, and got a lot of goals.' Chris Gibbons, stadium tour guide (2006)

'The first time [Seamus O'Connell] came down to play for Chelsea he came down on the train on the Friday to play on the Saturday and he had a brown paper parcel. And inside that were his boots. Extraordinary.'

Albert Sewell, Chelsea programme editor (2005)

below A final piece in the jigsaw was wiry, curly-haired inside-left Seamus O'Connell. He arrived as an unconventional amateur part-timer of Cumbrian farming stock, but proved a prolific marksman. O'Connell grabbed seven vital goals in his ten games in 1954–55, including a hat-trick on his debut in October in a 6-5 home defeat to Manchester United, this header in a 5-2 win at Bolton on New Year's Day and the winner at Cardiff on 23 March that sent the Blues top for the first time.

By the beginning of April teams such as Manchester United and Everton had fallen away and Chelsea's nearest challengers were Portsmouth and Wolves, inspired by England skipper Billy Wright. The Midlanders' visit on 9 April became something of a title play-off and was immensely tense for the huge and expectant crowd. Then, after 75 minutes, O'Connell's shot beat keeper Bert Williams and Wright, on the goal-line, fisted the ball over the bar (*left*). Incredibly, the referee initially gave a corner but was convinced after some minutes by the linesman that a spot-kick was the right decision. Reliable Peter Sillett drove home (*below*) for a priceless 1-0 win.

'I was on 36-hour leave from my national service at Catterick and managed to get to Stamford Bridge on Good Friday to watch the Wolves game in the Shed End … Billy Wright leapt to tip Seamus O'Connell's shot over the bar. Even though I was at the other end it was handball clear as day. The referee and linesman took an eternity to give it, and eventually Peter Sillett, silhouetted against the north end crowd, hammered it in. What a moment! There were 75,000 there that day, the biggest crowd I've ever been part of at the Bridge.'

Supporter Martin Dulcken (2006)

opposite Mastermind Ted Drake at his desk in Stamford Bridge's old ivy-covered offices.

'Years later I spoke to Peter about it. How did he feel? "I just hoped he'd keep to his decision and award a corner!" he said.'

Scott Cheshire, Chelsea supporter and historian (2005)

The championship rested on a win over Sheffield Wednesday at the Bridge. Considering the momentous occasion Ken Armstrong and Roy Bentley look relaxed as they prepare to leave the players' dressing room (*below left*). It was a turgid match but two goals from Eric Parsons (including this opening header, *below*), and another penalty converted by Sillett – this time debatable – gave Chelsea a 3-0 win and led ecstatic fans to chase the new title-winners off the pitch (*opposite left*).

'Chelsea are the greatest club I've known. The people here have taken it on the chin for 50 years and always come up smiling. That takes some doing.' Ted Drake, in his speech after winning the title (1955)

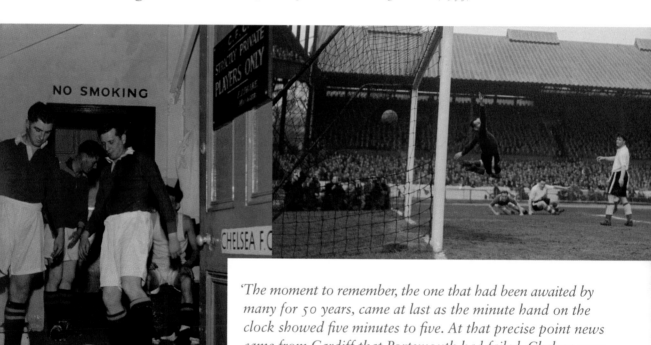

'The moment to remember, the one that had been awaited by many for 50 years, came at last as the minute hand on the clock showed five minutes to five. At that precise point news came from Cardiff that Portsmouth had failed. Chelsea were champions. And the 50,000 that had spent most of the afternoon giving advice freely – sometimes cynically, often wittily – to their heroes stood to cheer as history was made. Well, how have Chelsea done it? Mostly by team spirit, fitness and direct play, unlike the old dreamy Chelsea in the days of the Pensioners. They have collected 24 points out of their last past 16 matches Those figures have helped to put Chelsea at the top of English football. If not in style then at least mathematically.'

The Sunday Times (24 April 1955)

'They had wooden steps that went up from the pitch into the stands. But during the title celebration they'd pushed them to one side because the dog meet was to follow and they'd be in the way. So even while the club's celebrating they're preparing for the dogs!'   Joe Smith (2006)

'After the match people ran on to the dog track but the players went inside and had a drink of some sort. It was very low key. After a short while I just made my way home to Brighton and went to the Hove dog track to watch Bandits' Hut, a greyhound I owned, win. For winning the championship the board offered us £20, or a West End tailored suit. I chose the suit.'   Champion Stan Willemse (2005)

Chelsea's hard-fought run-in to the title went unreported in the press until late April because of a newspaper electricians' union strike. The headlines that greeted Chelsea's long-awaited triumph were worth the wait though. Manchester United, as in 2005, formed a guard of honour for the champions in the last game of the season and a banquet in honour of the success was held at Grosvenor House in Park Lane (*below*). Visible in the picture are secretary John Battersby (centre of first table) among former players, proud chairman Joe Mears, and the triumphant Chelsea team. The following season, the League trophy (*opposite*) was paraded round the Stamford Bridge pitch on a bizarre trolley as Chelsea hosted Newcastle United in the Charity Shield.

'It was so annoying that the newspapers were on strike and our progress at the top wasn't reported until towards the end. We didn't have a television, and radio didn't report sport anything like they do now. The Saturday evening newspapers were especially important to us – there were three in London then. I didn't blame the electricians who were on strike. I just thought it was typical of what always happens to Chelsea. It's always that way. When have we ever got any proper credit? All you heard was that we won with the lowest points total ever. I can remember them saying, "best of a bad lot". But that's because there were six or seven teams in with a chance of the title, including Man Utd and Wolves, and in my mind that made it harder than usual.' Chris Gibbons, stadium tour guide (2006)

'They didn't present the trophy on the day like they do now. Next season they paraded it round the pitch on a dressed-up wheelbarrow or something. Big flat thing it was. A club secretary walked next to it and some guards in uniform.'

Ron Hockings, Chelsea archivist (2006)

'So, 50 years of indeterminate struggle, of hopes and disappointments, of fickle behaviour have at last found a point of solid achievement. The taxi driver, the artist, the chimney sweep, and the actor, who have rubbed shoulders at Stamford Bridge can at last ride roughshod over the gibes aimed at "dear old Chelsea". Even the miniature figure of the footballer supporting the weathervane over the stand – some say it is a replica of Hilsdon, years ago the centre-forward of Chelsea and England – now has a new, purposeful look.'

The Times (25 April 1955)

When the Football League put pressure on Joe Mears, one of their committee members, not to accept the invitation to take part in the inaugural European Cup in 1955–56, the Chelsea chairman backed down and his club missed a golden opportunity. It would be another 44 years before the invitation came again. Nevertheless there were great nights – or afternoons – of European football on the usual friendly tours, and at the Bridge. In December 1954 Voros Lobogo (Red Banner), from Communist Hungary, were the feted visitors in a match for lovers of pure football broadcast live by the BBC. Led by withdrawn striker Nandor Hidegkuti and also boasting Lantos and Zakarias from the international team that humiliated England 6-3 at Wembley a year earlier, the Magyars played stunning modern football in a 2-2 draw. One move by the Hungarians, cooed one reporter, 'seemed to begin somewhere down the Fulham Road, wander off towards Fulham Road, and finally end in the Chelsea net.'

'There were 40,000 there, early on a Wednesday afternoon. If they'd had it on a Thursday, when shops had their half-day closing, it would have been even bigger – but the dogs were on Thursday afternoons. The Hungarians were a revelation. So much pass and move football, no long balls like English teams played. They always seemed to us to have three players round the ball at any time and their skill was incredible. Back then we'd never seen anything like it. Hidegkuti was just unbelievable: he was the captain and he was everywhere on the pitch. Still

opposite The visit of the Hungarians brought great football but poor spot-kicking. Three penalties (two for Chelsea) were squandered in the space of 11 minutes including Johnny Harris's second failure saved by Olah. Les Stubbs (*below*) had already driven home Bentley's subtle header to put the Blues temporarily 2-1 up.

Three years after Red Banner, the magic of floodlit football came to Stamford Bridge. Following a public trial match involving youth players (*below right*), Chelsea played Sparta Prague on the night of Tuesday 19 March 1957, the second half of which was transmitted live on ITV.

The Blues beat Czechoslovakia's champions easily, 2-0. The floodlight pylons, forming silhouettes on the SW6 landscape until the late 1990s stadium redevelopment, were as tall as Nelson's column and their 228 lightbulbs consumed half a million watts.

to this day he's the best footballer I've ever seen at the Bridge. It was a great game all round. We played well, especially Roy Bentley and Johnny McNichol. There were three penalties in the game and all of them were missed. John Harris missed our two. It had an impact on many fans. After we won the title and the Football League stopped us entering the first European Cup, Red Banner was the reason we were so gutted.'

Chris Gibbons, stadium tour guide (2006)

The Story of JIMMY *Greaves*

YOU want thrilling goals? Jimmy Greaves can dish 'em up. He's the lad with the lethal wallop, the snappiest chance-snapper in football. One of Ted Drake's greatest signings for Chelsea. A full England cap at 19, Jimmy's now 20. He looks certain to be in the headlines for a long, long time.

February 20, 1940. A happy day in the furnished rooms at Manor Park, East Ham, rented by James Greaves, London suburban train driver, and his wife Mary. For that day their first child was born—and christened James Peter.

From the time he could walk young Jimmy was kicking things around. Encouraged by his father, who'd played a lot of football in the Army, he was quite a nifty ball-worker by the time he was five. And much in demand at Huntsman Road, Hainault, to which the family had moved—because he was the only one in the road with a football.

When he was six, Jimmy shifted from Parsloes School to South Wood Lane School. There, though he was a tiny little chap, they made him a goalkeeper. Eventually he became a right-half—and then an inside-left.

Soon Jimmy was in representative teams—Dagenham Boys, Essex Boys, London Boys. What a great moment it was for his mother, too, to see her boy on T.V.—in a London Boys v. Manchester Boys match at White Hart Lane. London won 6-5. Strangely, Barry Sluman, who scored five of London's goals, and David Cliss, star inside-forward, were to become mates of Jimmy Greaves at Stamford Bridge.

Chelsea's scout, then, Jimmy Thompson—the man who is known by his bowler hat—was delighted when he read his evening paper. Sluman-Cliss-Greaves. All stars. And he had them all marked down for Chelsea!

Ted Drake wasn't able to follow up his title win, but arguably Chelsea's greatest home-grown player emerged in this period: Jimmy Greaves. The cartoon strip (*opposite*) shows his discovery by brilliant, eccentric Chelsea scout Jimmy Thompson. And in the image of his goal against Preston North End on the opening day of the 1959–60 season (*above*), we have his brilliant spell at Chelsea perfectly summed up: free-spirited, perfectly balanced, powerful and unstoppable, but ultimately frustrated – for despite his hat-trick against Preston, Chelsea could only draw 4-4. In the four seasons between 1957–58 and 1960–61 he scored 22, 37, 30, and 43 goals consecutively, but Chelsea finished 11th, 14th, 18th and 12th. To the fury of home fans Jim was sold to Milan in 1961 and returned only months later to join rivals Spurs. But Chelsea fans will never forget where he performed at his peak.

'*We started the training game and after about 20 minutes, this kid picked the ball up, started off on a run. Albert Tennant was the first-team coach at that time and he used to have one of these megaphones for shouting instructions, and he shouted "Get rid of it" and this kid went on and beat another one. "For Christ's sake, get rid of it!" And he went on and beat another one, and drew Reg Matthews out, who was an England goalkeeper, dipped his shoulder and Reg went that way and he rolled it in the far corner of the net. He jogs back to the halfway line and shouts out to Albert Tennant, "Albert – you didn't tell me when." Do you know who that was? Jimmy Greaves and I'll never forget. I played with Jimmy all the time he was at Chelsea and do you know, I still don't know whether he was left or right-footed! If you showed him the right, he'd go the right, if you showed him the left, he'd go that way, it didn't bother him. At 17 years old he played for us and scored five in a game twice. Absolutely fantastic goalscorer.'* Team-mate Frank Blunstone (2005)

1961–1970

Chelsea and the 1960s were made for each other. An explosion of new music, fashion and film was revitalising the old capital and nowhere was it more swinging than along the trendy King's Road, the Chelsea players' pleasure ground. Also in need of renewal was Chelsea Football Club as Ted Drake's star faded. In the six seasons since 1955, his team had not finished in the top half of the table, and the drop beckoned again…

Happily, at this time an astonishing array of home-grown young talent was breaking into the team, and a tempestuous young manager, Tommy Docherty, inspired them to promotion, the club's first silverware in ten years, near misses in the league, famous European nights and a first ever FA Cup final at Wembley. Great enduring legends of Chelsea came to the fore and the crowds flocked back. Like a storm, though, the Doc soon passed over in favour of

the calmer times of Dave Sexton, who moulded a side of flair and fight in equal measure and applied revolutionary techniques to training and match preparation. And under his studious leadership, at long last the FA Cup was finally paraded around west London in an open-top bus.

Ron Harris, who made his debut in 1962 and was a mainstay at full-back for the rest of the decade, was in a good position to observe the two managers' styles. 'Tom was a fantastic motivator of players and you knew how you stood with Tom. If he liked you, you had half a chance and if he disliked you, you were on your bike. If you played ball with him, Tom would play ball with you. Dave Sexton was completely different. Dave was a quieter fella but you knew when Dave was annoyed, just by him coming in the dressing room without saying a word, just by looking at his face. They are two of the best managers I ever played for at Chelsea.'

In September 1961, Ted Drake, whom history records as the only man to win the title for Chelsea in 99 years, left the club. He had six years left on his contract but 'the general lack of success' in converting a good young squad into a competitive senior one forced the board's hand. Chelsea had won the Youth Cup in 1960 and 1961 and been runners-up in 1958, and the phrase 'Drake's Ducklings' celebrated this success in the nursery. Among this 'golden generation' Terry Venables, Barry Bridges, Peter Bonetti, Bobby Tambling, Ron Harris, Ken Shellito and, soon, John Hollins and Peter Osgood, would all go on to represent England at international level.

below right Ted Drake's replacement was his recently appointed coach, the volatile young Scotsman Tommy Docherty. Although he could do nothing to stop the inevitable relegation in 1962, Docherty made changes and invested in youth, creating a bustling, passing side that took Division Two by storm. Leaders at Christmas, his novices' nerve was sorely tested by a minor ice age that suspended all league fixtures for six weeks. They survived a run of poor form to beat title rivals Sunderland and destroy Portsmouth to win promotion. It was the start of a swaggering, glamorous Chelsea that would win many admirers over the ensuing decade.

'The nickname was because of the way I used to scythe people down and that. That all came from Tommy Docherty because when I first went on the groundstaff I used to play as an inside forward. But when a manager comes up to you before a game and says, "When it's there you've got to bloody win it", you have that little bit of aggression in you. Then at the end of the game he comes round and says, "That's it, terrific." I'm trying to please the manager and I think that is how I got that little bit of aggression in me, through Tommy Docherty.'   Ron 'Chopper' Harris (2005)

left Ron Harris, Chelsea's all-time highest appearance maker, had his debut under Docherty in 1962. 'Chopper' went on to make 795 appearances, many of them as skipper, for the Blues before moving on in 1980.

'I went to Luton on Boxing Day and we won 2-0 on six inches of snow. It was our 11th game unbeaten and we were six points clear at the top. Then the freeze set in – others got league games in but we didn't. It felt like everybody was catching up. In the Stoke game manager Tony Waddington had brought a very experienced team and included Stanley Matthews. It was a bit of a lesson, men against boys, and Chelsea's nerves were obvious and Stoke won 1-0 in front of an enormous, very expectant crowd at the Bridge [below]. The match before, Leeds had drawn 2-2 at our place and the media had slaughtered us. I couldn't afford to go to the Sunderland match. It was live on the radio. My daughter has never forgiven me for that! Radio makes every attack sound like a goal. They seemed to have six corners in the dying moments and Bonetti performed miracles. I went through every emotion and frightened my daughter to death. When we beat Portsmouth 7-0 you realised this was still a great team.'

Chris Gibbons, Stamford Bridge tour guide (2006)

For 'Docherty's Diamonds' – as he himself dubbed them during a 1-0 FA Cup win over Leeds – the high-water mark was reached on 22 March 1965. At that moment his young side looked real contenders for a magnificent treble. A 3-0 win over Sheffield United left Chelsea top of the table with eight matches remaining having bagged the League Cup a week earlier and reached the semi-final of the FA Cup.

Chelsea had won the League Cup for the first time by beating Leicester 3-2 and 0-0 over two legs, with makeshift centre-forward Eddie McCreadie, usually a left-back, scoring a wonder goal in the first leg. It was the first silverware of the Docherty era. But then it unravelled. Five days later a muted Chelsea lost unluckily to Liverpool in the semi at Villa Park, with John Mortimore's opening 'goal'

disallowed for unfathomable reasons (*opposite left*). Sudden jitters in the league culminated in the 'Blackpool Incident' that ended all title hopes.

below Inside the Filbert Street dressing room, the players celebrate with the League Cup (left to right: Bridges, McCreadie, Upton, Venables, Murray, Boyle, Mortimore and Bonetti).

'I went to almost every game in 1964–65 aged 10, 11, and was convinced that would be the norm! I felt sure we were going to win the league, and we played some of the best football I've ever seen: wonderful, exciting, entertaining football. The League Cup wasn't that important then. I remember meeting a mate on the bus and he said, "By the way, we won the League Cup last night."' Andy Jackson (2006)

'We can't be champions this year, but we want to prove that we are the great side some people predicted we would be. I still feel it will be three years before we reach our peak. But who knows what will happen next year.'   Tommy Docherty (24 April 1965)

The league challenge ended in shame and division after the notorious Blackpool Incident. On losing 0-2 at Anfield (a match that could have put the Blues first), the Doc blew his top and cancelled a planned night out in the seaside resort. After training as normal on the beach eight senior players defied him and stayed out till the early hours. Docherty was fuming and sent them home the following day. The players united against the manager (*below right*) and released press statements in their defence, to no avail. So it was a scratch team that played in the crucial game at Burnley, and lost 2-6 – 'a sad ending to their eight months of ceaseless challenge in league and cup,' as one reporter observed. Had Chelsea won their final three matches rather than lost them, they would have won the league in 1965 by one point.

below Chelsea gained revenge for the 1965 FA Cup semi-final defeat by Liverpool, winning 2-1 at Anfield in the third round the following season. Osgood was the star of the show, but Tambling was on target with this long-range header for the winner.

'*Midway through the second half we broke from defence with a move involving all our forwards, starting with me out on the left. I played it inside to Terry Venables and then moved into the Liverpool half. George Graham was the last man to play the ball out on the right and he fired a deep cross into the Liverpool area. I jumped and sent a header looping into the net. While it wasn't a classic, what was so enjoyable was that it was the winning goal. We played them off the park and got what we deserved.*' Bobby Tambling (2002)

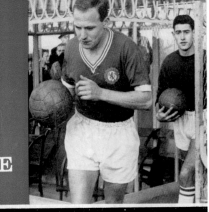

SPORTS ENTERPRISES LIMITED

left Chelsea capitalised on the King's Road fashion association with kit innovations. Docherty admired Milan's all-white kit and opted for all-blue, with go-faster stripes, at Chelsea. It went down brilliantly with fans and soon the club's first official outlet for replica kit was launched: youth coach Frank Blunstone's sports shop in Clapham Junction.

below Docherty was always unpredictable. The Scotsman accepted invitations worth £20,000 on behalf of his club to play two matches against the West Germans and assist in their 1966 World Cup preparations. Chelsea were chosen because their innovative overlapping full-backs made them the closest thing in Europe to Brazil.

'Tommy Doc opened the sports shop for us and we had Peter Bonetti working for us. We started a goalkeepers' pack – green shirt, green shorts, socks and green gloves – because "Catty" always wore gloves, and we sold hundreds of them, particularly at Christmas. Bobby Tambling advertised the boots for us. We were sending them to Australia, New Zealand, everywhere.'

Frank Blunstone (2005)

'We murdered them in the first game: I think we beat them 3-1. And the second game I think it was three apiece. And I'm talking about Beckenbauer and all of them, Uwe Seeler and Berti Vogts. It was some team. They were all young – 21, 22 – and the stadium was packed: there were fifty-odd thousand there. Great side. Great days.'   Tommy Docherty (1995)

'When we wore blue shorts for the first time against Villa at home [26 August 1964] it was a revelation – a major thing, so trendy. It was a different era: "swinging Chelsea". It was Docherty's idea. No one wore all one colour in those days. But it looked fantastic, so smart.'

Supporter Andy Jackson (2006)

Chelsea's consistency in the league earned European tournament football entry in 1965–66 for the first time since 1959. The Fairs Cup produced some memorable nights against the great continental names Roma, Milan and Barcelona. The first round tie with Roma will be remembered for the intensity of the violence on the pitch. The home leg, a 4-1 victory for the Blues, was dubbed the 'Battle of the Bridge' after fists flew and players from either side were sent off. The away leg, preceded by Italian publicity labelling Chelsea 'killers' and claiming the Roma chairman had been spat at in London, was a vision of football hell. Throughout the ordeal players were pelted mercilessly with fruit, bottles and pieces of metal and rubbish. Roma coach Oronzo Pugliese appealed unsuccessfully for calm (*below left*). Chelsea club medic Dr Boyne was hit by a balloon full of urine and, more seriously, John Boyle was knocked unconscious by a bottle as he prepared to take and throw-in. But Chelsea held their nerve and drew 0-0 to progress.

Wiener SK from Austria were dispatched 2-0 on aggregate in the second round and it was clear that players like Bonetti, Venables, Osgood and George Graham (*below right*, scoring in the 2-1 home win over Milan in the third round) in particular excelled in that environment. Munich 1860 were Chelsea's victims in the quarter-final, but it was Barcelona who eventually ended the Blues' hopes in a semi-final play-off when honours had ended even over two legs. *Opposite* Bobby Tambling (centre, falling) fires narrowly over the bar to the relief of Barcelona goalkeeper Reina, father of the present Liverpool keeper. Chelsea won the second leg 2-0 – a third on the night would have seen them through to the final.

'As the coach started to move, objects thudded against the windows and the sides of the bus. The women were told to get down on to the floor. Many of the players put up their bags as protection, and none too soon. As Eddie McCreadie covered his face, the huge window by his side exploded into a thousand fragments as a lump of iron tore through it. By the time the coach had whipped up to 50 miles an hour at least four of the so-called unsplinterable windows had been shattered. The driver had sense enough not to stop, as the rather shaken occupants shook themselves free of glass. Miraculously no one was hurt, but it took about ten minutes to get all the glass splinters out of the hair of Mrs June Mears, daughter-in-law of the chairman.'

Tommy Docherty on the journey from the stadium in Rome (1967)

left Super agile Peter 'the Cat' Bonetti, a youth team product, was Chelsea's number one for two decades, seeing off more than a dozen challengers, and bringing personality to the goalkeeping art with innovations such as the use of gloves and hurling the ball immense distances rather than kicking it. On retirement he served as Chelsea's first specialist goalkeeping coach.

left The result at Villa Park: Sheffield Wednesday 2 Chelsea 0. The limitations were starting to show. The FA Cup campaign of 1965–66 ended in more semi-final tears, for the wives of Messrs Bonetti, Tambling, Graham and co, as much as anyone else.

> '*Chelsea as yet are not mature or sophisticated enough to change their style to meet circumstance. Villa Park and Sheffield Wednesday found the cracks behind their wallpaper to prove that every match is different and that a side that can beat opposition like Roma, Milan, Munich, Liverpool and Leeds United – as Chelsea have done in cups this season – is not necessarily big enough to overstep a simpler-looking hurdle on another.*'
>
> The Times (25 April 1966)

below right Many fans' favourite, winger Charlie Cooke arrived as Chelsea faced Barcelona in the Fairs Cup in 1966. Cooke was intelligent, stylish and effortlessly skilful. It was said that when he conned an opponent with a body-swerve, they had to pay to get back in the stadium.

left No greater idol emerged from Chelsea's ranks than the King of Stamford Bridge, Peter Osgood. Ossie made his debut under Tommy Docherty in December 1964 and came to epitomise the talent and charisma of this young Chelsea side. Over ten years at the Bridge, he scored vital goals in Chelsea's cup triumphs and only missed the 1967 FA Cup final after breaking his leg the previous October at Blackpool.

below In 1967 Tommy Docherty, once more sacrificing 'brilliance for backbone', masterminded his first semi-final victory with the 1-0 win over Leeds. It was his £100,000 misfit, Tony Hateley (number 9, celebrating his goal), who earned the Doc his first FA Cup final with a jerked header from Cooke's jinking run and cross. Docherty and the players celebrated exuberantly on the pitch and on the train home (*opposite left*). Facing him in his first ever all-London affair at Wembley would be two former Chelsea favourites: Jimmy Greaves and the recently, reluctantly sold skipper Terry Venables. But Chelsea defeated themselves. Ridiculous disputes over players' tickets and bonuses marred an already inept preparation and the Diamonds shattered, losing 1-2 to Spurs.

'They say third time lucky and we proved that. People say Leeds scored a goal that was disallowed with the last kick of the game from Peter Lorimer's free-kick but I don't think anyone could begrudge us getting to the Final having played the semi-final the last three years. The Final was a real letdown because we were very poor on the day against Spurs. It was a very disappointing game all round.'

Ron Harris (2005)

The aftermath of the FA Cup final defeat was the end of Tommy Docherty. A tour of the Americas included a disastrous trip to Bermuda, where abnormal torrential rain delayed the three matches and confined the players to barracks. Tambling and Chelsea wowed locals with a 9-2 opener, watched by one in twelve of the island's population. But the final two games disintegrated into slanging matches and Docherty, incensed by Carlisle Crockwell's sending off of Hateley, abused the local referee before battling it out verbally with members of the Bermuda FA. The BFA reported his actions to the FA, who suspended the Chelsea manager from football for a month. Back home, Docherty felt he had no choice but to resign, and his brilliant, turbulent career at Stamford Bridge came to a sorry end on 6 October 1967.

'The Chelsea tour caused nothing but ill-feeling and can be best described as one of the biggest write-offs in the history of Bermuda soccer. Chelsea were nowhere near as popular as the day they arrived. They lost more popularity when Chelsea manager Tom Docherty verbally abused the referee before 2,000 spectators.'

Royal Gazette, Bermuda (June 1967)
Years later, Docherty returned to Bermuda, sought out Crockwell and apologised

IN MEMORIAM. CHELSEA Football Club
which died Oct. 6 1967, after 5 proud and
glorious years.—C.J.W.W.

The Times (11 October 1967)

Docherty's popular assistant, Dave Sexton, took his place. A pioneer in the use of technology, he used film recordings to aid match preparation. Sexton blooded the brilliant youngster Alan Hudson, brought in more dependable players such as Ian Hutchinson, Peter Houseman, David Webb and John Dempsey, and steered Chelsea to greater consistency and ever-improving league finishes of 6th, 5th and 3rd as the decade closed.

'I don't think I have ever been suspicious of glamorous or good players. The thing for a football manager to have is an eye for talent and there isn't anything better than that. So if you've got that you are a very lucky man. Basically we all went there, we rolled our sleeves up and we had a go and it worked very well. We had enough skill to give pleasure and we had enough hard work in us to fight for things. So it worked out okay.'

Dave Sexton (2005)

Sexton's crowning glory came in 1970 when Chelsea won one of the most memorable FA Cups in history. Chelsea had strolled through an all-London semi-final against Second Division Watford, winning 5-1 at Highbury, while gritty northern rivals Leeds United had played two scoreless matches before beating Manchester United 1-0 in a second replay. The fact that the final was between the King's Road swingers and Don Revie's arrogant Leeds United added colour to a fascinating epic for football fans of all clubs and anticipation was high. As in 1967, that most working class of Chelsea streets, Slaidburn Street, was decked out for the occasion (*below*). Pennants, banners and favours (*above left*) were shown off with pride and Chelsea issued commemorative cufflinks to the players selected for the match (*above right*).

'I remember walking round the World's End area before the cup final, lamp posts and kerb stones were painted blue and white, and there were banners all over the roads. It was far more community orientated in those days.'

Supporter Andy Jackson (2006)

FA Cup final morning was exhilarating for all Chelsea adherents bar one. Alan Hudson's injured leg had been in plaster until a week before the match, and the 18-year-old who had inspired Chelsea to the final missed out on a starting place. It was amazing that the violent challenges in the Wembley match that day didn't result in more players suffering Hudson's fate. On a playing surface ruined by a recent equestrian event Leeds led twice, and Chelsea replied, through the much-maligned winger Houseman and the fearless Ian Hutchinson's late header, to end it 2-2. The replay, at Old Trafford on a Wednesday night two weeks later, drew a record TV audience of 30 million. Again Leeds scored first, but Bonetti was in scintillating form and when Osgood (who had scored in every round) met Cooke's cross to beat David Harvey (*below*), Leeds visibly wilted. In extra time, Hutchinson's long throw was knocked in off his cheek by David Webb (*opposite*), who had been tormented by Eddie Gray in the first match. Chelsea had finally won the FA Cup.

'*This was not a classic. It was an epic.*'

Sir Andrew Steven, Chairman of the FA (12 April 1970)

below One of the most coveted mementoes in the late Peter Houseman's collection was his 1970 FA Cup winner's medal, which is now housed in the Chelsea Football Club museum at Stamford Bridge.

'I must admit I'd never been to Wembley, and I didn't go there focused – I got caught up in the occasion. I could have just as easily gone on the terracing. And Eddie Gray kept trying to take me on, he took it as a personal vendetta. I had never ever felt so knackered in all my life. I was telling myself I've got my bovver boots on for the second game. I made up my mind, there was no way anyone was going to do anything there, and I went out and didn't give a monkey's. It was the most fantastic atmosphere, the feeling there.'

Cup-winner David Webb (1995)

'The most fantastic thing was getting off [the train from Manchester] at Euston. I nearly missed the open-topped bus, because it started to move away and everyone was grabbing me, and I got caught up in the throng ... we'd been drinking on the train home, started drinking in the morning. Dave Sexton sat downstairs on the double-decker bus for most of the time. It was me that handed down the cup to the Chelsea Pensioners. The bus was stopped and there were all these crowds, and I leant down and nearly fell off the bus head-first, I was that drunk. A big fella, the chief scout there, Eddie Heath, grabbed me by the trousers.'

David Webb (1995)

below The team's open-top bus drove in celebration through the streets of Fulham and Chelsea. The biggest crowd was outside the Town Hall on Fulham Road (*opposite*).

1971–1980

Dave Sexton steered his all-star team to glory abroad in 1971 after some exhilarating continental travels in the Cup-Winners' Cup. Then in typical Chelsea fashion, just as the club looked set to take off, bad luck and errors of judgement set it on the road to ruin. The result was a decade largely to forget. The damaging break-up of Sexton's 1968–72 team and the doomed redevelopment of Stamford Bridge robbed Chelsea of experienced players and financial stability.

The club was relegated after 12 years in the top flight and the reputation for hooliganism meant that few lamented its fate. When the board's hand was forced to rest on the shoulders of a new crop of talented youngsters, amazingly, inspired by boss Eddie McCreadie, they temporarily restored Chelsea pride. But the sudden, inexplicable loss of McCreadie and his replacement with a series of unsuccessful managers left fans battered and bemused.

Looking back in 2005, with the benefit of 30 years' hindsight, John Hollins remembers why it all went right for a few years. 'Dave Sexton would be a fantastic manager in this era. He was always watching, learning, picking up different ideas. Back then, over 30 years ago, straight after the game, he would give us a chat, and then be out to Italy to watch a game on the Sunday, and be back on Monday morning for training. He would tell us, "I've found something else new. We're going to do this, or that." That's what helped us to win the FA Cup followed by the Cup-Winners' Cup.'

But Brian Mears, chairman from 1969 to 1981, sadly recalls the hard realities that followed those glory years. 'At that game [the 2-0 defeat by Tottenham in 1975], we had some really good kids coming up, and that's what I said to the board. I said, "We may be here a couple of years before we come back."

'"Oh, that long?"

'I said, "Well, yes, because next season we're going to be in the Second Division, I don't think with all the will in the world we're going to get promoted."

'And they said, "You're not saying you're chucking it in?"

'I said, "Of course not, I want to be promoted. I'm just saying that we don't have the players, we don't have any money, but we will do it because look at Ray Wilkins, Ray Lewington, Tommy Langley, Stevie Wicks, we still had Peter Bonetti…"

'We had the makings of a bloody good team.'

below One of the powerhouses of Sexton's sides was leather-lunged midfielder John Hollins, who managed a good haul of goals in his 592 Chelsea games. In August 1970, he scored what was dubbed 'the goal of the century', one that sent children out into the playing fields to imitate it for weeks. As the illustration from a contemporary book called *Golden Goals* shows, it was technique and athleticism that allowed him to cover the ground and control the rebound to win the game.

NELSON **1**

HOLLINS **1**

NELSON **2**

HOLLINS **2**

HOLLIN

'Always looking for a chance to strike forward from his linking position, Hollins cracks in more goals per season than many recognised attackers; and he is always looking for something special, often shots from way out that bulge the net to breaking point. But against Arsenal at Stamford Bridge, he surpassed himself. He broke forward on the left-hand side to chase a long pass from skipper Ron Harris. Though under pressure, he reached the ball before Wilson, and lifted it against the bar. Others might have stopped, but not Hollins; he beat everyone to the rebound and struck in a truly golden goal.'

Martin Tyler, *Golden Goals* (1972)

Two nights in Athens created Greek legends. Chelsea faced Real Madrid twice in the final and replay of the Cup-Winners' Cup on 19 and 21 May 1971. In the first game, though Sexton's men led through Osgood for 35 minutes, only heroics from Webb allowed the Blues to hang on through extra-time. The replay took place at the Karaiskaki stadium two days later, and around 500 of the original 4,000 Chelsea fans rang home to ensure work excuses were in place or extra money wired out. Sexton made plans of his own, switching from his usual 4-3-3 formation. Centre-half Dempsey, who had gifted Zoco for Real's 90th-minute equaliser in the first match, turned goalscorer in the second encounter, driving home the biggest goal of his career. Chelsea's second from Osgood was sheer class, one of his favourite strikes, live on BBC TV. The images of Sexton and the players cavorting on the pitch are etched in the mind of every fan who watched them. The World's End pub on the King's Road sold more than a thousand pints that evening.

'I was not satisfied with our attacking method in the first match against Real. Playing three up, against their back four, meant too much running for us in the humid conditions. I thought we could crack them in the replay by pushing up an extra player. This reduced our own running and they no longer had a spare man at the back. We really won because our two men in midfield, Charlie Cooke and Alan Hudson, outpointed their three.'

Dave Sexton (1971)

'The stadium's two electric scoreboards told the world that Chelsea had beaten Real Madrid, the old masters and Europe's most famous club, and won their first European prize.'

Albert Sewell, *The Chelsea Football Book No. 2* (1971)

'It meant more even than winning the FA Cup to me. It was virgin territory. This was the first time we'd ever got that far in Europe, so it was like we'd got to win it. And when we won it, [well-known supporter] Mickey Greenaway got over the fence, jumped a dry moat and got on the pitch. How he did it I'll never know – he was a big bloke. And he went up as they presented the cup on the pitch, snatched the cup out of Osgood's hand, kissed it and gave it back to him. Then they ran round holding the cup. That was Greenaway. He was in there. We couldn't even get over the fence!'

Garrison, long-time fan (2005)

The team had matured into a formidable one. McCreadie, Harris and Osgood (*opposite left*, in relaxed, airport mood), along with Dempsey, Webb, Hollins, Baldwin et al feared no one. As the teams saluted the fans at the end of the first game, Chelsea looked like winners (*below left*). In the replay big-game star Ossie netted the winner (*bottom*) and afterwards architect of the win Dave Sexton (*below*) cherished more silverware with John Hollins and Peter Houseman.

One of the last hurrahs of the Sexton era was the 21-0 devastation of Luxembourg part-timers Jeunesse Hautcharage over two legs in September 1971. It remains an aggregate goalscoring record in UEFA competitions, as does Peter Osgood's amazing personal haul of eight (*below left*, scoring number eight). Popular Tommy Baldwin, 'the sponge', scored four (*below right*, scoring number four). But the next round brought bitter disappointment with defeat at the hands of lowly Atvidaberg on the 'away goals' rule.

Much worse was to follow on 26 February 1972, just a week ahead of another Wembley cup final. A full-strength Chelsea side, including £250,000 signing Steve Kember, was cruising 2-0 against Leyton Orient, making a mockery of the Second Division club's pre-match boast that they might be outclassed, but they would exploit the Blues' complacency and win. Then after half-time, with Chelsea lethargic, a wonder goal by Phil Hoad, a second from Barrie Fairbrother (*opposite*) and a mix-up between Harris and Bonetti handed the Os a hardly believable quarter-final place against Arsenal. The alarm bells were deafening.

'I said to Peter Bonetti [after the first leg at Jeunesse], "I'll have a bet with you. I bet I score six goals at home." He said, "Right, you've got a fiver on." And on the night, I'd scored five and we had a penalty. And I was just going to take the penalty and there was a tap on my shoulder. It was Catty and he says, "Nah, Ossie, you don't take the penalties. Johnny Hollins does." So I said, "Hang on a minute, Catty ... " He said, "You're unprofessional, you are." I said, "Catty, we're winning 20-0, and there's two minutes to go ... " He said, "I don't care, Holly takes the penalties." And he took the fiver off me as soon as I got in the dressing-room.'

Peter Osgood (1995)

'I was a student, there were steel and railway workers, a hairdresser and a butcher. I remember we were really happy to be drawn to play Chelsea, a big London club. We never ever thought we would win the tie. The manager spoke to us before the game told us to try not to lose too high. The first leg was in Luxembourg. There were a lot of people at the stadium, 13,000 – the biggest crowd I had played in. It was a good experience even though we lost 8-0. We had a good time in London for the return, looking around, doing the sights. I think there were 30,000 at Stamford Bridge. It was a great atmosphere. We never thought they'd be gentle with us and they weren't – 13-0 there, and 21-0 overall. After the game there was a dinner, the players were great with us, and signed autographs. We really enjoyed the day. None of them said "hard luck" though!'   Guy Thill, Jeunesse Hautcharage midfielder (2006)

Few clubs have managed to exude glamour as Chelsea did between 1967 and 1972. An association with showbiz that extended back to the club's formation was celebrated in the programme in 1971–72 with the column 'Stars In The Stands', which featured, among others, supporters Ronnie Corbett, Arthur Askey, Bill Oddie and Judy Geeson (*below right*, who lived locally and brought cups of tea out to fans picketing the club to take Peter Osgood off the transfer list in August 1971). King's Road photographer Terry O'Neill brought the likes of Raquel Welch along too. Such a club had even George Best clamouring to play for it, and he finally fulfilled his ambition in November 1975 in Peter Osgood's Testimonial (*opposite, below left*). Even America's visiting Secretary of State Henry Kissinger (*below left*, along with June Mears, wife of Brian, and Labour Foreign Minister Anthony Crossland) would have needed all his skills in diplomacy to quell the increasing threat of civil war in the Chelsea dressing room. By 1972 the rifts were influencing performance – when Stoke City's old guard exacted a shock defeat in March's League Cup final thanks partly to a superb goalkeeping display from Gordon Banks (*opposite top*, challenged by John Dempsey), the stardust would take years to settle again. This despite the team's all-time great anthem 'Blue Is The Colour' reaching number five in the charts that same month (*opposite, below right*).

'*My guests at matches were mostly from the film world. I think I took Frank Sinatra once, I certainly took Laurence Olivier, Ralph Richardson, Johnny Mills, Kenny More, Jack Hawkins, Ava Gardner – she was a great pal of my wife. I think I took Duke [John Wayne] one time. On that famous occasion, though, Steve McQueen was my guest and said he wanted to meet the players. The managers have always been very sweet to me, Dave Sexton and Tommy Docherty especially. And at that time Steve was a god. So all you've got to do is say, "Steve McQueen would like to meet the players" and it happens.*'

Richard, Lord Attenborough (2006)

'I walked into the dressing-room one day [10 November 1973]. We beat Everton 3-1, I scored my 100th league goal, did a lap of honour, came in, and Richard Attenborough had brought Steve McQueen into the dressing-room. Michael Caine, people like that, you'd meet all the time through Chelsea.'

Peter Osgood (1995)

'When I told the Chelsea half that his Kop did him well he said, "They're only just starting on it really. It won't be finished until the end of the season." Good, goodness, gracious! It'll hold a mighty crowd when it is finished.'

Ernest Edwards, reporting Chelsea's first ever home match, *Liverpool Echo* (1905)

The youngest board in Chelsea's history embarked on ambitious redevelopment plans in 1972, but a combination of bad luck and planning and an economic downturn brought crippling delays to the construction work. Chelsea did not recover financially for two decades, and very nearly not at all. The first stand to be built at the Bridge was Archibald Leitch's classic East Stand in 1905. In 1930, and seemingly designed purely for greyhound meetings, the small, asymmetrical 'Shed' roof was built over the south terrace. The long-delayed but ramshackle North Stand was fully opened in 1945, and the West Stand in January 1966. The late-1960s board's ambitious vision of a new national stadium, including trendy restaurants overlooking Fulham Road, was scrapped in 1975.

above West Stand, built 1964–65.
right South Terrace, built 1930.

'*The old North Stand. When the trains went along the back there, that all shook. The stand shook.*'

Albert Sewell, programme editor (2005)

'*We shall change the atmosphere of the old stadium itself. Architects are working on plans for a modern cantilevered stand to enclose the big terracing opposite the players' tunnel. That will alter the whole climate, shrink the place psychologically and give it all the sense of urgency the game and its players need.*'   Tommy Docherty (March 1965)

'*Others have built new stands, but this will be a totally new stadium. When it is finished Stamford Bridge will accommodate 60,000 people under cover with two thirds seated, and the capacity itself could be increased to 80,000 should there be a call for it. Chelsea will never be the same again.*'

Chairman Brian Mears, launching the East Stand development (1972)

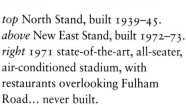

top North Stand, built 1939–45.
above New East Stand, built 1972–73.
right 1971 state-of-the-art, all-seater, air-conditioned stadium, with restaurants overlooking Fulham Road... never built.

However, the dream was partially realised in the modern development of 'Chelsea Village', with its hotels, restaurants, nightclub and fitness centre in the 1990s.

When the players he brought in, such as Keith Weller, Chris Garland and Steve Kember, failed to click, and when established stars including the demi-gods Cooke, Hudson and Osgood would no longer perform for him, Dave Sexton's days were numbered. There were disputes right through this period. Sexton's innovations, including pitchside half-time talks such as this one against Norwich in 1972 (*below right*) no longer inspired his players. Cooke quit in 1972, only to return two years later. 'King' Os had put in a transfer request in May 1967 and was listed for sale by Sexton at a British record £250,000 in August 1971 for 'lack of effort and doing less and less' which prompted massed fan protests (*below left*). But when he, Bonetti and Hudson were disciplined over Christmas 1973–74 the heart of the team was broken in its prime and the break looked permanent. Within days Huddy had moved to Stoke, while the board publicly backed Sexton. In March Ossie joined Southampton, and by the end of the season Webb was a QPR player. In October 1974, Dave Sexton, Chelsea's most successful manager, was sacked. The golden age was over. But a new golden boy, Ray Wilkins (*opposite*), quickly emerged.

'The squad at that time was one of immense talent. Dave Sexton had that side, and you walked into the dressing room, and you looked around at the faces, and you thought: "I don't think I should be in here." To get on the same field as them, you thought, "This is wonderful."'

Ray Wilkins, remembering his debut, aged 17, in October 1973. 18 months later he became Chelsea's youngest ever captain (1995)

'For the away game at Sheffield United on New Year's Day, Dave Sexton attempted to reverse the team's decline by dropping Bonetti, Osgood, Hudson and Baldwin, and in effect signed the death warrant for the Chelsea we once knew. Both Osgood and Hudson protested by refusing to train with the first team. The club suspended them and put them both on the transfer list. I read with alarm the soggy, cliché-strewn announcement in the Derby County programme, "There comes a time in everyone's life – at work, within families, in sport – when there is a clash of personalities, and it is evident that for some time such a situation has existed at Stamford Bridge between the manager and one or two players." Hudson went to Stoke, Osgood went to Southampton, I carried on buying the programmes. But I can't pretend my confidence wasn't dented.'

Supporter Giles Smith, *My Favourite Year* (1993)

From the deluge of relegation in 1975 sprang hope from the usual source: youth. For the crucial dogfight at Spurs near the end of that season, lost 0-2, caretaker manager Ron Suart appointed Chelsea's youngest ever skipper, the prodigious midfielder Ray Wilkins. Not even the genius of 'Butch' could save Chelsea from the drop but the feeling grew that a fresh young generation might return soon enough. When left-back Eddie McCreadie took over the helm in the Second Division he opted for youth and tenderly eased out his old team-mates. He created a bustling, short-passing side in which Wilkins was the maestro, fed by the scurrying Ray Lewington. The promotion campaign of 1976–77 was sensational and the fans' relief (*below*, McCreadie is mobbed after the season's final home game

'*McCreadie: that was such nonsense. He got them promoted and then all this argument over a car or something. He wanted a better car and they stood up against him and that was the end of him. Having taken them up in some style, out of a lot of young players, I thought he was entitled to see what he could do next and I think they threw it away there. [Danny Blanchflower] was bewildering. I don't think the players knew what he was on about half the time, in tactical stuff. Geoff Hurst was another one that didn't work out.*'

Albert Sewell (2005)

against Hull) at such a short stay down below understandable. But then, shockingly, a contractual dispute between board and manager ended with the inspirational McCreadie walking away. His successors – Ken Shellito, Danny Blanchflower (*below left*), Geoff Hurst – were unable to make the team greater than the sum of its parts and didn't last long. Still there were some standout games before the inevitable drop in 1979, not least the unforgettable win over Liverpool in January 1978, when the new generation forwards Clive Walker (*below*, scoring the first of his two goals), Tommy Langley and Steve Finnieston took the reigning English and European champions apart 4-2 in the FA Cup.

'I'm 20, it's my first FA Cup match, 42,000 crowd, I'm playing against the England goalkeeper, and I score in the 14th minute. I'd gone past Joey Jones, looked up, got to the edge of the box, saw the goal, and thought if you can hit a good shot you've got a chance. I hit it well, with pace, and Ray Clemence couldn't read the flight of it or thought it was going wide. People say "what a great goal" because it moved in the air like you can't believe. The crowd went absolutely ballistic. My sixth goal in seven matches. My second that day, Ian Britton put a great ball out to Bill Garner, and I knew he'd hold it up. A little touch from Bill, and I just knocked it in.'

Clive Walker, scorer of two goals in the 4-2 cup win over Liverpool (2006)

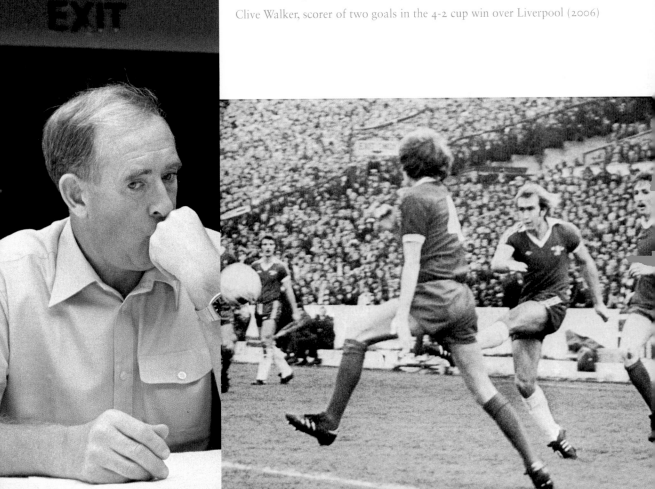

1981–1990

A decade of change began poorly and went rapidly downhill, with an unprecedented fall from grace in the league only narrowly avoided. Off the field, the behaviour of some fans plumbed new depths and the Mears family's proud three-quarter-century association with the club ended in shame and recrimination. Worse, concern over the stalled stadium redevelopment was eclipsed by Chelsea's disastrous financial state, and soon the very real prospect emerged of its ancestral home, Stamford Bridge, being bulldozed for housing and shops.

But an aggressive new chairman, Ken Bates, an experienced manager and a shrewdly bought-in team eventually revived the sleeping giant. Amazingly, Chelsea became a force again. Long-suffering supporters, many of whom were digging deep into their own pockets to help keep the club afloat, decided to organise themselves to have a say in the way the club was being run.

Martin Spencer, then Chelsea's chief executive, was withering in his criticism of the late 1970s board: 'I think the club was run as a social club instead of a business. Very few positive decisions were taken and we just shilly-shallied from crisis to crisis.' In contrast new chairman Ken Bates was determined to turn things around: 'We are not going to fold because I enjoy football too much. When a great club, which is what Chelsea are, has become worn around the edges, tatty and decayed, improvements are going to take time, but we now have the organisation to make the gradual changes we are looking for.'

Disgruntled supporters mobilised to have a say in the running of the club, and no one felt more at home among them than Pat Nevin, one of the great stars to emerge in the mid-1980s: 'It kind of sums up how I felt about Chelsea that I remember a game against Liverpool when David Speedie scored the opening goal, and I missed the game through injury, so I did what I thought was the natural thing: I went and stood in the Shed. Not one person said hello. Stood there the whole game and not a word was said. Dozens of people were looking and shaking their heads: "No, it'll not be him." I loved it. And it was fantastic to go and watch a game in the Shed. It was almost a metaphysical thing with me and Stamford Bridge. I was at home on every inch of that ground. I never felt that at any other place.'

Reporter: 'Do you realise that Chelsea will be more expensive than Manchester United next season?'
Ken Bates: 'Yes, but look what you can save on the train fare.' Press conference (1982)

Bates inherited John Neal (*below right*) and Ian McNeill (*below left*) but liked the cut of their jib and, typically, stuck by his management team when the fans had turned against them and players such as Alan Mayes, Chris Hutchings and keeper Steve Francis, who struggled to make an impact in the Second Division. The anti-Neal protests of March 1983 (*opposite left*)

followed a successful clamour for chairman Brian Mears's head two years earlier. Fans were determined not to sit back in silence and let Chelsea fail.

At the end of that 1982–83 season, Chelsea faced relegation to the Third Division, and possible oblivion, should they not succeed at Bolton's Burnden Park. On a tense, drenched afternoon, winger

Clive Walker scored one of the most important goals in the club's entire history (*opposite right*) and disaster was averted.

The Chelsea team that secured a 1-0 win that day was Steve Francis, Chris Hutchings, Gary Chivers, Mickey Droy, Joey Jones, John Bumstead, Mike Fillery, Colin Pates, Bryan 'Pop' Robson, Clive Walker, Paul Canoville.

'It was the 1982–83 season and the football was shocking. At one game we started chanting "Neal out!" We started on the benches and got moved on. More "Neal out! Neal out!" We got shoved out of the Shed, and a few hundred of us ended up, after the game, doing a sit-down protest in front of the old Shed turnstiles, singing, "Bring back our Eddie [McCreadie] to us!" Bates spent some money the following summer. Of course Johnny Neal did the business after that – great times – and proved us all wrong. Suddenly we were all, "Johnny Neal, Johnny Neal, Johnny Neal!" That's football fans for you!'

Chris Carver, supporter since 1968 (2006)

The sign that shows the mood at Stamford Bridge.
Picture: PHIL SHELDON

Fans angry as Chelsea swing by a thread

Chelsea 1   Rotherham 1   By MARTIN MARKS

CHELSEA fans looked on in anger as their side continued to nosedive towards the Third Division.

With just three matches to go, the prospect of this once-swinging club playing the likes of Wimbledon and Port Vale is a very real one.

They will need a dramatic improvement against Sheffield Wednesday tomorrow to give themselves even a slim chance of avoiding relegation.

Dejected manager John Neal, well aware that its his head the Chelsea fans are demanding, said: 'Relegation would be nothing short of degrading for us'.

Top of the table

	P	W	F	A	Pts	GD
QPR	38	24	70	31	78	+39
Wolves	39	20	62	37	73	+25
Fulham	39	19	61	43	66	+18
Leicester	39	19	68	41	65	+27
Newcastle	39	16	66	50	60	+16

'The fans were fantastic, cheering throughout the game. I ran over with Mike Fillery and Clive, took our shirts off and threw them into the crowd as a show of thanks. When we got back to the dressing-room the manager asked us where our shirts were. We said we'd chucked them to the fans and thought no more about it – until we found the cost of a shirt had been deducted from our wages.'

Gary Chivers (2005)

Ken Bates, the man who would have most to say about Chelsea's next 20 years, had become owner of the club at 8.45a.m. on April Fools' Day 1982. It was an appropriate date given what he was taking on. The club was losing £600,000 a year and had been relegated in 1979 with its worst-ever points total – 20 – and things had barely improved under experienced manager John Neal. On the terraces a hard core of followers continued to make 'Chelsea fan' synonymous with 'hooligan'. Bates was determined to challenge this head-on while vigorously defending the well-behaved majority, and tried to attach an electric wire to the fences around the ground in 1985 (*opposite left*). The controversial move angered fans and was blocked by the GLC on safety grounds. Terrace bigotry was another problem. Racist groups like the NF actively recruited at matches, their magazine *Bulldog* openly sold outside Stamford Bridge. Other teams featured black

*'I remember being involved in a bundle with someone in the West Stand because not only was he bedecked in Nazi memorabilia but he was shouting the most obscene racist comments. "Go and ****ing shout somewhere else mate,' I told him, "I've come here to watch the football, not listen to your crap."'* Tony Banks, Lord Stratford (2005)

below The infamous North Stand ruckers move in on Liverpool supporters during the 1982 FA Cup match. A scene typical of the days before the tragedies at Heysel and Hillsborough.

players, but not Chelsea. That is until 16 March 1982, when Paul Canoville (*right*) made his debut against Crystal Palace. While warming up the winger was racially abused by his own fans. Happily, the man who became known as King Canners ignored them, worked hard and established himself as a popular first-teamer.

'[Canoville] was the club's first black player and, inevitably, immediately became a target of the crop-haired, heavy-booted National Front membership among his own crowd. Those Chelsea "supporters" believed they would hound him out. The rest of the crowd looked on without demur, deaf to the "monkey" insults. In response, some of us sponsored items of Canoville's kit in a match programme feature. It was a small gesture, but a way of demonstrating that not all of us harboured such malevolent instincts.'

Journalist Nick Townsend (2004)

Neal and McNeill clung on and Chelsea were transformed in 1983 by the arrival of several shrewd signings, surging back to the First Division in fine fashion. The crescendo of hope and expectation carried on into the new season especially after a thrilling draw at Highbury, in which goal machine Kerry Dixon (*right*, after scoring against Arsenal) and David Speedie (*opposite*, netting in the thrilling 5-4 Full-Members Cup final win at Wembley against Manchester City) ran Arsenal ragged. Chelsea really were back with a vengeance. With those two, tricky Scots winger Pat Nevin (*centre*) formed a mesmeric and hugely entertaining triangle of attack. Here was a team of big personalities and indomitable spirit. There was no better example than the unforgettable League Cup

comeback away to Sheffield Wednesday in January 1985, from 0-3 down to leading 4-3, after the inspirational Canoville was introduced at half-time. It ended 4-4, but the club was finally going places again. The first senior silverware for 15 years was won in 1986 – albeit only the Full-Members Cup. More importantly, the Blues finished sixth two seasons in a row – tellingly, the highest finish since 1971.

'*Rougvie picked out Dixon, the archetypal big blond, with a swift free kick. Though his shot was blocked by Jennings' foot it fell kindly for him and he hit it back past the goalkeeper with the eagerness of a good forward.*'

Clive White, match report of Arsenal 1 Chelsea 1 (27 August 1984)

'We hated each other. We were opposite
characters. He was really volatile, and I was
quite laid back. But I didn't like his methods
of trying to be in control of me and my play.
He was doing it, because he wanted the ball
as often as possible – even more than Kerry!
What made it particularly difficult was that
my understanding with David was probably better than the understanding I had with any other player in my life. I knew where he was
all the time. And I knew where he was going to go. After a few years
we actually became good mates. We got to know where each other
was coming from. And finally clicked.' Pat Nevin (1995) on team-mate David Speedie

'*Peter Langan saw the paintings for sale, and he knew I was a big Chelsea supporter, so he bought them for the brasserie. And when he put them up, he said, "They're yours when you retire." But he died before I retired, so I never got them. George Graham wanted to buy them. Ken Bates was after them for a long time. And each time they were told to ask me, as if they were mine. They all used to come to Langan's: the Mearses, Bates, Trevor Birch, Colin Hutchinson, Gwyn Williams, Tony Banks, David Mellor. Managers too: Ruudi used to come in, Vialli, Bobby Campbell, Peter Shreeves. Gwyn always introduced me as "the top man in London". It was a lot of old bull**** but it got him anything he wanted. Ossie, Huddy, Hutch – we had a benefit do for Hutch at Langan's when he was ill. Lots of agents too. That was all through me. To some people they weren't anybody, but to me they were the bee's-knees, they were Chelsea people.*' Michael Henry, executive club member and former maitre d' of Langan's (2006)

opposite This painting is one of two by Laurence Toynbee of Stamford Bridge that hang inside Langan's Brasserie near Green Park in London, for many years a 'Chelsea restaurant'. It shows the moment when training, under the watchful eye of the coach and a director or two, was finishing and the dog track was being set up.

below Paul Canoville scores 10 seconds into the second half to begin one of the greatest comebacks in the club's history in the Milk Cup fifth round replay at Hillsborough in 1985.

'There wasn't a lot John Neal could say. He just made a substitution and shuffled it around a bit. Colin Lee made way for Paul Canoville, and Dale Jasper moved to centre-back. It was one of Chelsea's most inspired replacements ever … And of course, playing down the hill, straight from kick-off, Canners runs through and scores. Suddenly they're thinking, "**** me – what's happened?" The game completely turned on its head. Our support was absolutely fantastic and the momentum was with us. Before you know it we're 4-3 up, and then Big Doug brings Mel Sterland down – the only player on their side still capable of getting over the halfway line. But it was okay, because we beat them at home. It just would have been a lot quicker if they hadn't got that penalty.'

Nigel Spackman describes the legendary 4-4 against Sheffield Wednesday (2005)

These metal badges are a selection from the many collected by writer and Chelsea season ticket holder Simon Garfield and his son over the years. The very earliest badges sold at football grounds in the 1930s were made of plastic, with a slot to pop in the portrait of your favourite star.

'The Pensioner badge, that's my favourite and the most popular. Chelsea are the Pensioners, whether they like it or not. People still say, "Who're they, mate, in the red coats?" I'm still using the same die for that and it's 60 to 70 years old. A die's a terrible lot of money today; £150 down the drain. It didn't cost that much money then. It's very heavy, solid iron, and it shapes the metal for the badge. Now that is the foundation. Then when you've stamped out three or four hundred badges with the die, you put it to one side and put a number on it – god knows how many dies I've got! You can reproduce years and years later the same thing. Then it's a finishing process of putting colouring in, varnishing, polishing, putting the pin on the back.'   Joe Smith, supporter and badge maker since the 1930s (2006)

When Bates bought the club for a nominal £1, the draining £1.6m debt with Barclays from the eight-year-old East Stand was separately vested in SB Properties, owners of the freehold on the ground and Chelsea's landlord. Eleven acres of land in the west end of London is always attractive to predators, but the 1980s was the age of the developer, and the SB Properties shareholders, chiefly David Mears, decided to sell the ground for housing and retail. Bates bought into SB and started a nine-year guerrilla war on their property developers, Marler Estates (later Cabra). The expense and the uncertainty restricted the club's planning and once again the Chelsea faithful were asked to raise money for the 'Save The Bridge'

fund (*below right*, launched by Bates, Colin Hutchinson and David Mellor) – a similar 'Cash For Chelsea' scheme had been launched in the mid-1970s. Meanwhile, John Hollins succeeded John Neal as manager following his heart problems in 1985. The sureness of touch of Hollins the player was not evident in his unsuccessful spell in charge and Chelsea looked

rudderless. The spirit of political activism was everywhere in 1987, and a group of frustrated fans launched the left-wing *Chelsea Independent* (*opposite*) which aimed to make representations on behalf of supporters to those running their club, on squad strength, transfers, ticketing and the behaviour of some fans, notably the terrace racists.

'I remember how difficult things were when I was manager. Once I couldn't believe how long the grass was getting. I asked why it hadn't been cut and was told they owed money on the mower and weren't allowed to use it. I gave the groundsman £50 of my own money and told him to go out and buy anything that would solve the problem.'

John Hollins, Chelsea manager 1985–88 (2005)

'I gave evidence at the public inquiry. I also saw one or two of the people from Marler – there was a guy called John Duggan, and I said to him, "You know, I don't think you have any idea what forces you're letting loose here, of the venom that will be directed at you." And he said, "Oh, in every village where we try to develop there's always some brigadier who doesn't want it." I said, "You better pray to every god you know that you're never asked to find out what our brigadiers are really like!" I always assumed that if it did require several thousand Chelsea fans to descend on that site to make a nuisance of themselves, they would have done that.'

David Mellor, 'Save The Bridge' campaigner (2006)

'[Supporters are] being asked for £15 million to "Save the Bridge". We believe that Chelsea fans should get something in return for their money. We already spend thousands of pounds a year in following Chelsea, and yet we have no say whatever in decisions that are taken by the club and which affect us more than anyone.'

Chelsea Independent, issue one editorial (May 1987)

Even though there was obvious discontent under Hollins, no one imagined such a talented team could draw so many winnable games – 15 at home. Bobby Campbell, the man Ken Bates said would never manage Chelsea, replaced Hollins in March, but he was unable to avoid the drop. It was facilitated by the novelty of a play-off system in which the team in 18th place in the First Division battled it out with the also-rans of the Second. A bizarre goal by Charlton's Paul Stewart earned the draw at Stamford Bridge that threw the Blues into the maelstrom, just when Gordon Durie's opener (*below left*) looked to point the way out of this unexpected nightmare. Horrible performances away (0-2) and at home (1-0) to Boro sealed Chelsea's relegation. At the Bridge, the last charge of the hooligans (*below*) earned the enforced closure of some stands for the first six home games in Division Two. Over the summer Campbell rebuilt Chelsea as a promotion SWAT team, drilled by inspirational former Rangers defender Graham Roberts.

'If it hadn't been for the Heysel tragedy, we would have been in Europe in 1985, and who knows how far we would have gone? But at the end of that season there was a change and John Hollins took charge. We had a few problems: the influx of new players unsettled things, and what was looking to be the start of a big, big castle being built was blown away in a matter of months. The departure of Mickey Thomas and the appearance of Jerry Murphy on the scene completely baffled most punters, I would imagine. But there you are: managers see things differently, and that's how things are done.'

Gwyn Williams, Chelsea management staff 1979–2006 (1995)

The skipper's 15 strikes (12 of them emphatic penalties) and the rejuvenated Dixon's 25 helped earn 96 goals and 99 points (then a record) as Chelsea stormed back to the top league as champions (*below*, with Durie, Roberts and Peter Nicolas propping up their manager). Dixon's goals, and shrewd buys, such as keeper Dave Beasant and stopper Ken Monkou, helped secure a creditable fifth place in Division One as the decade closed. It included a hugely enjoyable league win at Highbury with John Bumstead's goal – the last until 2006. After that there were no more relegations. By 2006–07, only six Premiership teams had survived longer among England's elite.

'We had a really nice bunch of lads with some good characters. Some of them liked a drink and we could celebrate everywhere, but we also worked very hard. We were the best team in the league, but the best team doesn't always win the league. We were tight at the back but also played entertaining football. Our nearest rivals were Manchester City and they had lost 3-2 to Walsall. We had to go there a few days later [in February 1989] and all the Walsall people were telling us how they would do the same to us as they had done to City. We beat them 7-0.'

Graham Roberts, Chelsea captain (2005)

1991–2000

After the grind of the 1970s and 1980s, the 1990s was a wonderful decade of renewal and reward. The battle to keep the Blues at the Bridge was won, but how would the club thrive in peacetime? With Glenn Hoddle kick-starting its radical modernisation and a wealthy new benefactor in the wings, the club was transformed by a landmark decision in 1995 to gamble on fast-tracking Chelsea to stand among Europe's elite. Soon some of the great names of continental and British football were arriving – including the maestro who would be voted Chelsea's greatest ever player – and money was also found to rebuild the decayed stadium.

'What an exciting place it is, Chelsea,' enthused Graham Rix, a member of the management team between 1994 and 2000, 'even the quality of kit! The training pitches are immaculate. The whole place is just a professional football club, as it should be. They have not got one excuse at Chelsea Football Club. Any player who comes here gets well looked after medically – massage and everything is top-notch. It's all laid on. If he cannot produce the goods, that's not our fault. We've taken the pressure off Chelsea Football Club and put it back on the players.' Hoddle left to manage England but his replacement, the incomparable Ruud Gullit, won the coveted FA Cup in his first season. Wembley

hero Roberto Di Matteo, whose goal after 42 seconds epitomised the hunger and quality of the new Chelsea (*below*), couldn't remember anything about the goal after the match: 'It was so quick, after that I was so excited. I was so carried away I just couldn't calm down and it was unbelievable, the feeling, and also so great an emotion for me. I think it's the first time I've felt something like that.'

Inevitably Chelsea still produced shocks, none greater than the death of wealthy and popular supporter Matthew Harding and the departure of Gullit. But there was sustained success at last, home and abroad, under new boss Gianluca Vialli, and Chelsea had once again become the home of 'sexy football'.

Bates's stealth finally won the battle with the developers at Stamford Bridge in 1992, to the relief of all associated with Chelsea, but what of the club's health? Soon after a spectacular 0-7 defeat at Nottingham Forest, Bobby Campbell made way for Ian Porterfield, leaving a squad of big personalities under a novice manager. Dennis Wise (*right*) shed the baggage of playing on the wing for Wimbledon to command the centre of Chelsea's midfield for 11 years. Also in that promising side were keeper Dave Beasant, imperious centre-half Paul Elliott (*opposite*), hard-man Vinnie Jones, Ireland's World Cup star Andy Townsend (*below*), and great Chelsea juniors Graham Stuart and Jason Cundy. On 1 February 1992, former Dons Wise and Jones stuck a note on the 'This is Anfield' sign saying, 'We're bothered' and took that attitude to Liverpool, scoring a goal each and beating them 2-1. It was Chelsea's first league win there since Harry Burgess's winner at Christmas 1935. The following month, though, a great chance to reach the FA Cup final was squandered against Sunderland, and Porterfield was blamed.

'Reds Mugged By Crazy Gang.'

Liverpool Post & Echo headline (1 February 1992)

'Nobody really appreciates how important it was, getting the ground, because that was the basis upon which everything could take place. We couldn't develop the ground. It was owned by somebody else. And the Royal Bank of Scotland was fabulous, they gave us a 20-year lease with an option to buy any time at a fixed price, and that was December 1991. In 1993 we started to build what was later to be called the Matthew Harding stand.'   Ken Bates (2005)

'I played against Chelsea for Newcastle and they were a very big side. They had Vinnie Jones, Ray Harford, Tony Cascarino. They were physical and played a very long ball game as well. There are certain clubs you associate with attractive football and my belief of history was that Chelsea was an attractive football team with glamour and sex appeal. I don't think the club was going in the right direction.'

Gavin Peacock, who joined Chelsea in 1993 (2005)

'Paid him to do his best.
Stood his ground.
Done the test.
Then told to p*** off like the rest.'
Dave Webb's off-the-cuff ode to managing Chelsea (1995)

When Porterfield's bright start collapsed in two winless months from December 1992, Bates looked to a Chelsea hero, FA Cup winner and former Southend boss David Webb (*right*) to end the dangerous wobble. Webb's pragmatic, psychological approach steered Chelsea to safety. He left with heartfelt thanks and Glenn Hoddle, who had surveyed the Chelsea scene while recuperating from injury there a few years earlier, accepted the challenge. Hoddle wanted root-and-branch change: from the Harlington training ground where students shared dressing rooms with Chelsea players and where transfer negotiations were conducted over a payphone with the money-box removed, to players' lifestyles and healthcare and the quality of the football played. 'Master the ball,' he said, 'or the ball masters you.' The board backed this brave new world and invested in players such as Gavin Peacock and Mark Stein – whose record scoring sequence from Christmas 1993 of nine goals in seven games stiffened support for the Hoddle project.

'To be honest, I didn't really enjoy the football in the first two years, apart from the cup run, but the final year was completely different.'

Glenn Hoddle (1996)

opposite Glenn Hoddle, with assistant Peter Shreeves (left) and physio Bob Ward.

'When I came to Harlington we had a little pokey dressing room for the first team and a rota where on Monday it might be my turn to bring in the biscuits and Tuesday it might be Wisey's, then after training we'd come back in, drink tea and dunk in the biscuits. Of course, we think about it now and laugh but it isn't the best way to deal with your body after you have just trained. Afternoon training sessions were unheard of and Glenn used to do that. His pre-seasons were different. They weren't one of those where you'd go around and do loads of cross-country runs and that. All those different types of philosophies he'd try to bring in and without a doubt I feel I was here at a turning point in the club's history.'

Gavin Peacock on Hoddle's impact at Chelsea (2005)

Although Chelsea struggled to 11th in 1993–94, they completed a stunning 1-0 league 'double' over title-winners Manchester United, both winners scored by elusive midfielder Gavin Peacock. Having beaten Luton Town – featuring emotional old boy Kerry Dixon – in the semi-final, United lay in wait in the FA Cup final. After Peacock's wicked long-range drive struck the bar and out, Chelsea's first FA Cup final in 24 years succumbed to the wretched weather and similar refereeing by David Elleray. There were two penalties in a 0-4 drubbing. The silver lining to Wembley's storm clouds was qualification for European competition for the first time since 1971–72, and despite UEFA rules restricting the quota of non-English (as opposed to British) players in Chelsea's side, Hoddle steered the Blues to the semi-final, where Real Zaragoza, inspired by Gustavo Poyet, eventually ended the dream. But along the way there were memorable European nights, such as the overcoming of Bruges at the Bridge, and the valiant 1-1 at Austria Memphis, where Scots striker John Spencer ran 80 yards to score an unforgettable goal (*opposite*).

left Player-manager Hoddle applauds the drenched Chelsea fans at Wembley after coming on as a second-half substitute in the dispiriting 0-4 FA Cup final defeat of 1994.

'They made a defensive mistake at one of their corners and I was offski. As I received the ball, I looked about, took two touches from the box and I was over the halfway line. I just knocked it forward and tried to get into my stride as quickly as possible. I was worried about the hamstring, but I looked around me and saw there was nobody anywhere near me, and there was no need to go any quicker. And there was these big mad Austrian plodders running after me, going "Rooarrr!" like six Erland Johnsens with black hair. And I just remember as I was running seeing, I think it was a black hand, out of the corner of my eye – and it was Eddie Newton's. I looked round and he's galloping like a madman. I thought, "Jeezus, he's crackers!" And I was saying, "C'mon, keep up with me, keep going." And the keeper's seen me looking, and I've faked the shot and he went one way and I put it into the net.'

John Spencer on his Austria wonder goal (1995)

The Cup-Winners' Cup gave the Chelsea board a glimpse of what might be. To raise funds they decided, fashionably, to float the club on the AIM, a sub-market of the London stock exchange, as part of the new 'Chelsea Village' complex. It coincided with the intervention of Matthew Harding, a multi-millionaire and fervent Blues fan who had wooed wife Ruth with midweek matches and a bag of chips along the North End Road. Harding's timely injection of cash helped Chelsea's massive new stadium redevelopment and enabled ambitious plans to be scripted in the so-called 'Marriott Accord' of 20 May 1995. At a Heathrow hotel on the morning of the Everton-Manchester United FA Cup final, Bates, Harding, Hoddle and chief executive Colin Hutchinson decided to spend big and turn Chelsea into a major European club. The result was an amazing influx of stars from across Europe, including Mark Hughes (*opposite below right*), Dan Petrescu and the biggest signing in Chelsea's history, the charismatic Ruud Gullit (*opposite left*). Gullit succeeded Hoddle as manager in 1996 and the strategy continued, bringing in, among others Gianluca Vialli, Gus Poyet, Tore Andre Flo, Roberto Di Matteo, Frank Leboeuf, and, of course, Gianfranco Zola (*below*), the genius who transformed Chelsea's image and would, in January 2003, be voted the greatest player in Chelsea's history.

'I gave Chelsea fans what they wanted, a dream. And they gave me what I was dreaming of, too. It was a complete relationship, where I was giving and I was receiving. And I think for them it was the same. It was like the best marriage you can have.'

Gianfranco Zola (2003)

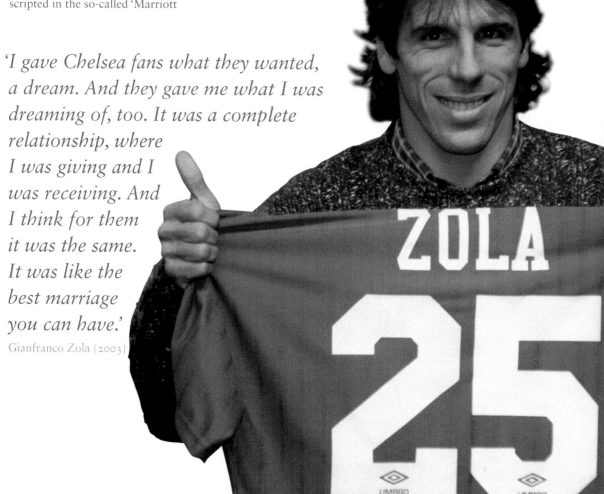

'*I was the driving force because I could see that football was changing dramatically. At that stage I didn't know how dramatic it would be with Bosman. European competition, we'd had the taste of it and it was obvious that at that stage we were on the level of Crystal Palace and Queens Park Rangers and we had the opportunity, the ground was now secure, Matthew was now around, we were getting things together. We would probably never have that opportunity again and we had to grab it with both hands or, really, accept that we were going to be just a middle of the road club hoping that we would stay in the Premier League, hoping that we might have the occasional cup run, but not really having any ambitions above that. Or we had the opportunity of trying to break in.*'

Colin Hutchinson (*above right*),
former managing director (2005)

'*They don't need to be helped, they settled in quite well. Their English is getting very good. I've taught Luca a few phrases – they're all fluent Cockneys now, which is good.*'

Skipper Dennis Wise on the continental influx (1996)

Gullit's continental collection started to play modern, attractive, expansive football, and he continued the revolution off the pitch in diet, training and facilities. They took many teams apart including Derby, 4-0, at the Bridge, when Gullit coined the phrase 'sexy football'. But the defining moment of his reign came in late January 1997 against Liverpool in the FA Cup. Two-nil down, at half-time the Dutchman unleashed the raging bull Hughes and asked Di Matteo to man-mark John Barnes. It worked brilliantly, producing one of the most thrilling comebacks in Chelsea's history, a 4-2 slaughter to match the deafening atmosphere, in which Hughes, Petrescu, Zola and Vialli were mesmeric. It was the first time Liverpool had lost from a 2-0 lead since 1964. The FA Cup looked destined for Chelsea – particularly poignant since the shocking death of super-supporter Matthew Harding (*below*) a few months earlier in a helicopter accident on the way back from a match at Bolton.

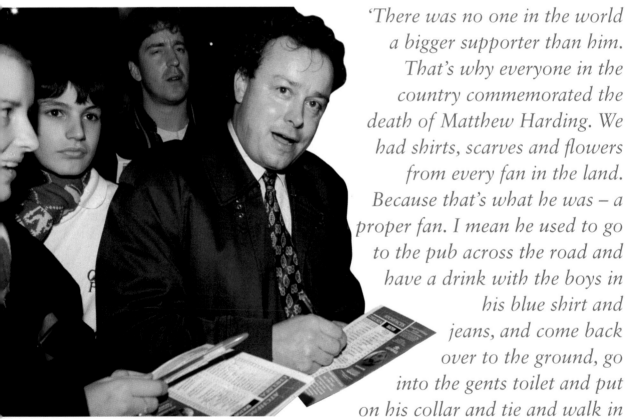

'There was no one in the world a bigger supporter than him. That's why everyone in the country commemorated the death of Matthew Harding. We had shirts, scarves and flowers from every fan in the land. Because that's what he was – a proper fan. I mean he used to go to the pub across the road and have a drink with the boys in his blue shirt and jeans, and come back over to the ground, go into the gents toilet and put on his collar and tie and walk in for his directors' lunch.'

Michael Henry, friend of Matthew Harding (2006)

left Hughes ... 1-2.
above Vialli ... 3-2. The great 4-2 turnaround of 1997 against Liverpool will be remembered for a very long time.

'I reckon the second half against Liverpool when we came back from 2-0 down was the best 45 minutes seen at the Bridge since our great days. We contested five major finals in eight years, and I'd like to think these lads can do even better than that.'   Peter Osgood (1997)

'A lot of people looked at Matthew and thought, this guy is not wholly in control of himself. I was very sad and upset when he died. Matthew was a guy it might well have been possible to pull back. Everyone goes through phases of thinking they walk on water. Matthew might have grown out of it; sadly, we'll never know.'   David Mellor (2006)

'I get a lot of satisfaction when I hear people behind me screaming their delight for this sexy football. The good thing is we now know we can play like this.'

Ruud Gullit, after the 4-0 demolition of Derby (29 November 1996)

Boasting a galaxy of star names, in 1997 Chelsea finished a creditable sixth in the Premiership and surged to the FA Cup on waves of public sympathy over Matthew Harding and affection for the little magician, Zola, who was named Footballer of the Year, despite joining the Blues three months into the season. But in the final against Middlesbrough it was another Italian who stole the show. Cultured midfielder Roberto Di Matteo stunned everyone by striking the fastest-ever FA Cup goal after just 42 seconds. Di Matteo's blind sister was in the stand; afterwards Dennis Wise kidded her it was he who'd actually scored it. Eddie Newton, a rare and popular home-grown in the side – Gullit's 'silent force' – scored the second (*opposite*). It was Chelsea's first major silverware for 26 years and the celebrations on the pitch lasted 45 minutes. Gullit was hailed as the first black manager to win the famous trophy.

'Matthew Harding has been with us in spirit all season.' Ruud Gullit (17 May 1997)

'Before the kick-off on Saturday I said to Dennis Wise, "Let's make sure that after this game they're all talking about the team from the 1990s and not the 1970s." It's so nice to finally put an end to all that stuff. It was great for the guys who did so well for the club in 1970 but it had gone on far too long. It had become like a huge weight on our shoulders but we've finally laid this ghost once and for all. Now, with the quality we now have in the side, it's important we go on to bigger and better things. We don't want to wait another 26 years for our next trophy.' Steve Clarke (18 May 1997)

'You try and run a replay in your mind. Middlesbrough had kicked off confidently enough and moved out to the right. Somebody lost it and suddenly [Roberto Di Matteo] was haring down on us, ball at his feet, Mark Hughes charging to the side as a decoy. The shot came in laser-straight to the roof of the net. This was death. Those opening minutes were truly terrible. From where we sat at pitch side, the tension in the Boro players was almost tangible, the confidence singing from Chelsea feet. Hardly a red-shirted touch worked properly. Those cosmopolitan sophisticates in blue seemed to be running a masterclass. Petrescu to Zola to Hughes to Wise to Di Matteo. A skilful web of Europe spread across the pitch. For Chelsea this was fulfilment. For Middlesbrough you felt it could only get worse.'

Brough Scott, sports writer
(18 May 1997)

From the first days of the *Chronicle* Chelsea's programme has always set the trends and sold more than most. This spread provides a sample of different styles over the years.

'It was 16 pages of all football for 6d. And they started on Christmas Day, 1948, Tommy Walker's farewell match. A proper programme. But the Evening News *gave them hell about doubling the price. "It's outrageous and it'll never last."'*

Albert Sewell, programme editor 1948–78 (2005)

1905–06

1933–34

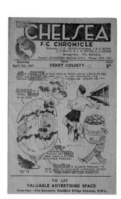

1946–47

1947–48

1948–49

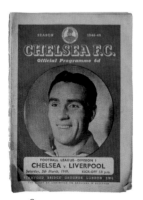

1948–49

1949–50

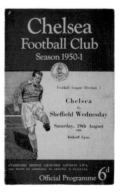

1950–51

1950–51

1951–52

1957–58

1959–60

1962–63

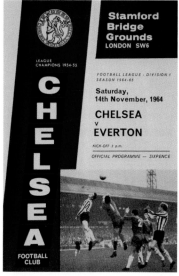

1964–65

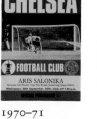

1970–71

1975–76

1984–85

1985–86

1986–87

1987–88

1991–92

1998–99

2000–01

2002–03

2003–04

2005–06

When Ruud Gullit left Chelsea after negotiations over his 'netto' salary collapsed, the well-liked Gianluca Vialli became Chelsea's third successive player-manager. Despite finding the transition from the players' best friend to their boss difficult, the former Italy international won an incredible treble in his first year in charge. In the 1998 League Cup, Di Matteo, again, and great servant Frank Sinclair, beat Boro 2-0, again. The Cup-Winners' Cup final in Stockholm, invaded by Chelsea fans in what was said to be the greatest (fogbound) airlift since the Cold War, was Zola's night. He'd been injured and travelled back to Italy to regain fitness. But he was kicking his heels in frustration on the bench until the 70th minute, when he was brought on. He instantly latched on to Wise's through pass, and volleyed into the net past the Stuttgart keeper for the winner. Four months later, it was the deadly drifter Gus Poyet who scored the solitary goal against Real Madrid in the UEFA showcase, the Super Cup. In six and a half months, Vialli the novice had won more silverware than any manager in Chelsea's history. He won the FA Cup again in 2000 but that still wasn't enough to keep him in the job.

Three's up for Vialli in 1998: former Chelsea junior Frank Sinclair matched his 'Blues Brothers' mate Eddie Newton by scoring at Wembley in the 1998 League Cup win (*above*), the genius Gianfranco Zola came off the bench to win the Cup-Winners' Cup (*right*, with Vialli), and goalscorer Gus Poyet, the cunning Uruguayan, was at the centre of victory celebrations in Monaco for the Super Cup (*opposite*).

'This is the greatest moment of my life. This is amazing, I can hardly believe it. To be honest, I was surprised I wasn't playing because I have worked so hard to get myself fit. Perhaps I was a little bit frustrated, but I was able to turn that into a positive because when I came on, I was tuned-in and spot-on. I deserved it for the passion and work I have done in the last 18 days.'

Gianfranco Zola (14 May 1998)

'I have to say thank you God for this victory because I know I've been a very lucky person lately, and I really mean that. Also I know I've not been easy to get on with as a manager and I would like to thank all the players and staff at Chelsea because I've been a pain in the backside sometimes. People say football is only a game, but to me it's a matter of life or death. It was a great night when we beat Stuttgart, but I'm never satisfied – if you become too complacent in this game, you will never win anything again.'

Gianluca Vialli (14 May 1998)

The squad had been strengthened every year – World Cup-winners Marcel Desailly and Didier Deschamps pre-eminent – and competed in every competition. In 1999 third place in the Premiership was the club's best finish since the days of Dave Sexton. The Champions League, though, was this side's arena, and in October 1999 Chelsea's thoroughbreds thrashed Galatasaray 5-0 in Turkey and drew 1-1 in a match of the highest class at the San Siro. Dennis Wise's late equaliser from Di Matteo's dazzling pass against AC Milan (*below*) is still serenaded at matches. And how Stamford Bridge throbbed the following April, when Chelsea purred and Barcelona were taken apart 3-1, with Tore Andre Flo unstoppable. The return leg, lost 1-5 by Vialli's subdued team, showed how much work still needed to be done at all levels at the club. They were not champions material yet.

'At Chelsea we all were desperate to win the league title. The fans loved the cup and we did the best we could in all competitions. But we couldn't win the title and that hurt, so we had to make sure we did as well as we could in the Champions League and qualified for it every season.' Gustavo Poyet (2006)

Champions League thoroughbreds: (*bottom*) Wise, Deschamps, Flo, Albert 'Chapi' Ferrer, and Emerson Thome hail opening goalscorer Zola (centre) during the momentous 3-1 home win over Barcelona in April 2000. In the same campaign, the record-breaking 5-0 drubbing of Galatasaray in Istanbul came despite 'Welcome to the Hell' banners and an intimidating police presence (*below*). Home fans applauded Chelsea from the pitch afterwards. On-fire Flo scored twice in both these games.

'We were in Italy for the Milan game, sitting outside a coffee bar, and one of our group got up and started singing to two attractive Italian girls. Paul, this guy's manager, was trying to make him look a bit special. He gave me a napkin and said, "Go and get his autograph and pretend you don't know him, he's going to be big one day." Yeah, yeah, I thought and strolled over and got him to sign it as if I was a complete stranger. I remember telling Paul as I sat back down, "He's no good, he'll never make it, and that hat looks ridiculous." I still have the napkin to this day. It says, "Best wishes, Craig David"!'

Peter Trenter, Chelsea Supporters Group (2006)

2001–2006

The world, for Chelsea fans, stood still for the five seconds it took Frank Lampard to run the ball towards the Bolton goal, sidestep Jaaskelainen and pass the ball into the net to make it 2-0. For the first time in half a century, Chelsea were champions. Fast forward twelve months, and the same goalscorer stood in the same spot, as he reminded us in his celebration, well on the way to back-to-back title wins. Rewind three years and Bates's ambitious Chelsea Village development was not the banker he'd predicted and the club was in serious financial difficulty.

'You never quite knew with Ken Bates whether he was going to slap you on the back, insult you, or ask you for £10 million,' jokes multi-millionaire supporter Peter Harrison. It would take the arrival of the 'billionaire from nowhere' and the 'special one' to produce the winning formula. Chelsea became a club that would take on the mightiest in the world, that could recruit almost any player it wanted.

There were controversies, and abuse from clubs and fans whose pitch had been invaded were loud and prevalent. But to real fans Chelsea was not, as the detractors claimed, a club with 'no history'. It was the same old 'moneybags Chelsea' of 1910 again, splashing the cash and bound for glory. Except this time the joke was not on the misfiring Blues, but their outpointed rivals. 'I have many much less risky ways of making money than this,' said Roman Abramovich, echoing the words of Gus Mears nearly a century earlier. 'I don't want to throw my money away, but it's really about having fun and that means success and trophies.'

'He brought some great players in and something from day one last year felt right, it felt special. From that moment the manager was in charge, we knew.'

John Terry on José Mourinho's instant impact (2005)

By 2003 Eidur Gudjohnsen and Jimmy Floyd Hasselbaink had a prolific strike partnership, but arguably the goal that was most important to Chelsea's destiny was a rare one by Marcel Desailly, on Sunday 11 May that year against Liverpool. It was the strike that won the point that earned the place that put the crucial Champions League cash in the bank. Financially, the match was so important that worried chief executive Trevor Birch made a Henry V-style rallying speech to the players before the game. Birch was actively seeking new investors at the time. Two months later, Roman Abramovich saw enough potential in Chelsea to buy the club lock, stock and barrel.

'I think it meant everything to the club to win that game. Who knows whether Mr Abramovich would have been as interested if we hadn't have been in Europe? I said [to the lads] that there are only a few times that your character is really tested: this is one of them. This could be the difference between staying at the top table of football or drifting into oblivion. Now is the time for you boys to step forward and prove your worth.'

Trevor Birch, chief executive (2005)

'I was never really close to taking over. When I sold my computer business in 2001 Chelsea asked me to get involved but I couldn't get over the lack of transparency whenever I asked for details. I have great respect for what Ken did, but his plans depended on the football club being successful at the very highest level, and failure to sustain European success was what cost the club dear. You look at the UEFA Cup disappointments of St Gallen, Hapoel Tel Aviv and Viking Stavanger, and they meant probably £30 million-odd was lost to the club in revenue it should have had. There were big names there on hefty contracts, and I had to be convinced my investment would have a "dynamic effect", i.e. take it forward. So to save my concerns, instead of getting involved and worrying, I decided just to watch and enjoy the football.'

Peter Harrison, another potential investor (2006)

below Manager Claudio 'Tinkerman' Ranieri, Vialli's successor in September 2000, steered an impressive course in the Premiership but flopped in the UEFA Cup between 2000 and 2003. For Bates (*opposite*) it was time to cash in his chips, even though Desailly's vital equaliser against Liverpool (*centre*) secured the financial safety net of Champions League football for 2003–04.

On Thursday 26 June 2003 Chelsea entered into discussions with Roman Abramovich and his aides; by Tuesday 1 July the deal to buy Chelsea Football Club was done. Mr Abramovich's team conducted an instant assessment of the club, and soon found among the playing staff the foundation for a team to challenge the best in the land. It immediately became clear this was no arms-length proprietor: Roman Abramovich (*left*) would attend every game, and virtually kick every ball from his box in the West Stand.

'Growing up at Chelsea, I was very lucky to have two great captains behind me to learn from. Wisey was totally different to Marcel, really vocal and noisy around the place, playing jokes and you know the things he did for the lads on and off the pitch. Marcel had that presence where he didn't need to shout and when Marcel spoke everybody listened.'

John Terry on his captaincy training (2005)

'We signed the agreement eight to eight-thirty at night. Ken Bates had left. Not much of a celebration. I walked home from Stamford Bridge. Two of my sons were home. I said, "I've just represented the Russian gentleman who's bought Chelsea Football Club." They said, "Sure you did!" "No – watch it on the news." They watched and were dumbstruck.'

Bruce Buck, season ticket holder and future chairman, on the deal that changed football forever (2006)

Two peerless centre-backs would step out of the shadow of 'The Rock' Desailly to make Chelsea's the best defence in the land. Youth team graduate John Terry (*opposite*, standing his ground with Bradford's Dean Windass under Desailly's watchful gaze) and William Gallas, who became a France international at Chelsea. Although Desailly and Gallas (*left*, overpowering Dennis Bergkamp) starred in the 2002 FA Cup final at the Millennium Stadium, Chelsea lost disappointingly 0–2 to Arsenal following Terry's overnight illness.

'I was in America on holiday, in LA, in a shoe shop. My dad rang me and told me. It's funny, I remember it exactly: it was a big thing, a billionaire taking over. But you didn't know how free-spending he would turn out. I just remember being in a cab with my missus after, and discussing it, a mixture of amazement, happiness and a bit of worry.'

Frank Lampard on the moment Roman Abramovich bought Chelsea (2005)

Chelsea's original 1905 jerseys were Eton blue, the horse racing colours of club president the Earl of Cadogan, and a lighter hue than now. Royal blue was adopted around 1912. From 1909, Chelsea's goalkeepers wore contrasting jerseys to distinguish them from other players. Badges didn't feature on players' shirts until 1961. The first sponsor's name, Gulf Air, appeared on shirts in the 1983–84 season.

(Home colours unless stated, a = away shirts, 3 = third-choice kit.)

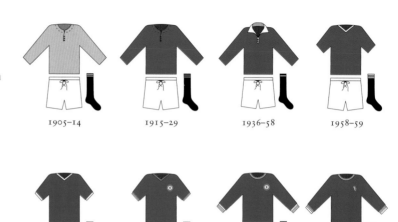

1905–14   1915–29   1936–58   1958–59

1959–60   1961–62   1962–63   1964–66

1966–72   1967 *semi-final*   1967 *final*   1970 *final replay*   1972–75   1975–77

1977–81   1977–81 a   1981–83   1981–83 *a*   1981–83 3   1983–85

1983–85 *a, 3*   1984–86 *a, 3*   1985–86   1985–86 *a*   1986–87   1986–87 *a*

1987–88 3

1987–89

1987–89 *a*

1989–90 3

1989–90 3, *a*

1989–91

1990–92 *a*

1991–93

1991–93 3

1992–94 *a*

1993–94 3

1993–95

1994–96 *a*

1995–97

1996–98 *a*

1997–99

1998–2000 *a*

1998–2000 3

1999–2001

2000–02 *a*, 3

2001–03

2001–03 *a*, 3

2002–04 *a*, 3

2003–05

2003–05 *a*, 3

2004–06 *a*, 3

2005–06

2005–06 *a*

2006–07

2006–07 *a*

'Within six weeks I think I'd spent more than any other chief executive had spent in his entire life. I think it got to about £120 million.'

Trevor Birch (2005)

Once Abramovich was in charge, he embarked on the biggest act of wealth redistribution in world football: Damien Duff (Blackburn Rovers) £17 million, Hernan Crespo (Internazionale) £16.8 million, Claude Makelele (Real Madrid) £16.7 million, Adrian Mutu (Parma) £15.8 million, Juan Sebastian Veron (Manchester United) £15 million, Wayne Bridge (Southampton) £7 million, Geremi (Real Madrid) £6.9 million, Joe Cole (West Ham) £6.6 million, Glen Johnson (West Ham) £6 million, Alexei Smertin (Bordeaux) £3.5 million. The investment brought immediate returns, not least Crespo's crafty equaliser at Highbury in October 2003. Claudio Ranieri, initially laughed at for his lack of English, managed Chelsea to their highest finish in 49 years.

'I went to the press conference for Veron and Joe Cole. I was pretty impressed, as a Chelsea fan. That was a real excitement for me. When the team came back from Malaysia, I was having a drink with Trevor Birch in Fishnets, when Geremi came over and chatted to us, and I thought, "This is pretty good."'

Bruce Buck, Chelsea fan-turned-chairman (2005)

'It makes me laugh when United fans complain about Abramovich when, in fact, not so long ago they were the ones dangling huge contracts and nicking the best players from smaller clubs: Roy Keane, Gary Pallister, Paul Ince, Brian McClair, Neil Webb... these were the Wright-Phillipses, Parkers, Coles and Duffs of their day.'

Gabriele Marcotti, journalist, broadcaster and Chelsea season ticket-holder (2005)

'I know when I came for the pre-season, a lot of people said, "He came for money." Money is important but if it was only money, I would have gone for another club. When I wanted to leave Real Madrid, Chelsea told me they had a big project and had ambition. I like this.'

Claude Makelele (2005)

opposite Meet some of the new boys, Mr Ranieri. Wayne Bridge, Glen Johnson, Damien Duff, Marco Ambrosio and Geremi show how some of the summer 2003 cash was spent. Argentina striker Hernan Crespo proved that money can buy you love with his crafty long-range library-silencer against arch-rivals Arsenal in October 2003 (*below left*). But no Abramovich recruit proved more pivotal than midfielder Claude Makelele (*below*).

The sideshow to developments at Chelsea was whether 'Tinkerman' Claudio Ranieri, mocking himself as a 'dead man walking', would be replaced. When Chelsea overcame Arsenal in the Champions League quarter-final, courtesy of Wayne Bridge's unforgettable strike, he cried with emotion. But the tears were his players' when Chelsea disappointingly failed to see off Monaco in the semi-final.

Euro ups, Euro downs. Left-back Wayne Bridge's 87th minute winner at Highbury in April 2004 (*above*) earned Chelsea a Champions League semi-final place at only the second attempt. But opponents Monaco rallied after a controversial sending-off in the principality, Ranieri's tactics didn't work, and Monaco finished the job at Stamford Bridge despite the dynamic Frank Lampard (*left*, eluding Monaco's Prso) putting the Blues in the driving seat at 2-0. Blowing such a great chance of reaching the coveted final was too much for many of the players, including Gudjohnsen (*right*, comforted by Monaco boss and former Chelsea midfielder Didier Deschamps).

right For all Carlo Cudicini's quality in goal, 22-year-old Petr Cech's arrival in 2004 set the seal on a formidable Chelsea defence. His concentration, dominance and agility earned worldwide acclaim, and in his debut season he would manage 23 Premiership clean sheets, eclipse Peter Schmeichel's record for not conceding a goal with a new high of 1,025 minutes, and concede just 13 times in 35 matches.

'As soon as it left [Wayne Bridge's] boot I shouted "Gooaal!" and grabbed the nearest person on the shoulder and shook them, quite violently, probably, until it hit the net. People were jumping around everywhere in sheer ecstasy. Some nutters were standing on top of the backs of seats and just jumping anywhere, just for joy. It was mad.'

Supporter Damien French on Bridge's Champions League quarter-final winner at Highbury (2005)

'I knew the club had big potential to be one of the best. When I signed the contract, they were still in the Champions League and playing fantastic. I was watching the game against Arsenal and when they went through to the quarter-final in the last minutes, I saw this was a big moment.'

Petr Cech, signed for £6.5 million in January 2004 (2005)

'It was a great night for the whole of Chelsea and I'm ecstatic. It's the best night of my career and a lot of the lads are saying the same thing. He's [Ranieri] a good man and deserves a lot of credit for the way he has handled himself. All the speculation isn't nice and he has done a great job.'

Frank Lampard on the Highbury high (7 April 2004)

Champions League-winning coach José Mourinho joined from Porto in the summer of 2004 and the team was transformed, especially with the arrival of keeper Petr Cech, winger Arjen Robben, striker Didier Drogba and defenders Ferreira and Carvalho. By Christmas Mourinho's men were six points clear at the top of the Premiership.

'Totally organised. Very thorough. Always expects improvement from everybody, whatever job they do in the club, because we can always learn and always improve and he's also of that mind. His professionalism. Dedication to detail. The way that he knows how to laugh and joke with players, but also how to motivate them.'

Gary Staker, team administrator, on just what makes José special (2005)

'It wasn't till after that I got home and saw it and thought, "What a goal." I was buzzing to score against such a great team and get the winner.'

John Terry on his Barcelona goal (2005)

By March they had outpunched Liverpool in the League Cup final at Cardiff, and by April Chelsea were champions again after a 50-year wait, this time with a record 95 points. In the Champions League, after controversial refereeing by Anders Frisk in the Barcelona away leg, Chelsea stormed past the Catalans 4-2 with a Stamford Bridge match the equal of any in the great old stadium, only to lose to Liverpool, a team they had beaten three times that season, in the semis.

'I am not one from the bottle; I am a special one.'

José Mourinho announces his arrival at Chelsea (August 2004)

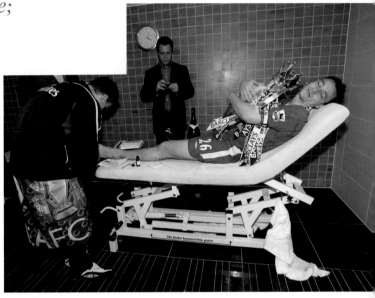

'It was strange. It took a while to sink in. Just amazing. Shaking the champagne and shouting and screaming, and then after the game you have a moment when you sit on the coach and think, "Oh Jesus, we've won the league." And to give it back to the club I adore and love – that's not only great for me but everyone here.'

Eidur Gudjohnsen (2005)

Under Mourinho's (*opposite top*) shrewd management, the entire squad became heroes when they won the League Cup in February 2005 by beating Liverpool 3-2 for the first silverware of the Roman Era. But it was close friends, captain and vice-captain, John Terry (*opposite bottom*, heading his remarkable winner against Barcelona) and Frank Lampard (*left*, notching his famous second goal against Bolton to seal the title), who came to embody the Champions of 2004–05: mentally and physically strong, professional, skilful, intelligent: exceptional. Lampard broke the Premiership goalscoring record for a midfielder with 19 in 2004–05 and 20 in 2005–06, and was runner-up to FIFA World Player of the Year Ronaldinho in December 2005. Both he and Terry have now won domestic Footballer of the Year awards. JT played out the last match of the 2004–05 season against Charlton barely able to walk but, through sheer bliss, wouldn't let go of the Premiership trophy, even on the treatment table (*above*).

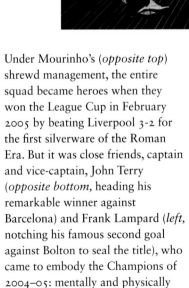

José Mourinho always talks about the emotional response to an event, and he need never have doubted his squad after the title win – even new boys Essien, Wright-Phillips and Del Horno. A best-ever start of nine straight wins set the foundation for a smooth run to the championship. Again Europe provided special moments, including a 4-0 ravaging of Real Betis, but when Chelsea met Barça this time, the sending-off of Del Horno in the first home leg effectively sealed the tie, despite a valiant rally. The media had turned against Chelsea's dominance and the spring left the team's step. League 'doubles' over Arsenal, torn apart by Didier Drogba, and Liverpool, similarly shredded by Joe Cole, were the league's hors d'oeuvres before the decisive 3-0 win over Manchester United, Cole again the assassin with the final bullet. Amazingly, José Mourinho threw his medal into the Matthew Harding Lower end – honouring Chelsea's most fervent fans. And with that, Chelsea became only the 11th team to retain the title in 130 years of English football. Like the surprising last chapter of a roller-coaster novel, it was an unbelievable ending to a century of ups and downs.

below The all-star cast of Lampard, Cech, Essien, Gallas, Huth, Robben, Geremi, Makelele, Duff, Carvalho, and powerhouse Didier Drogba savours the moment after dishing out Liverpool's worst home defeat for thirty-six years, the devastating 4-1 win of October 2005. The 2006 title race decider with Manchester United was a joyous walkover. Joe Cole capped his fantastic campaign with a virtuoso goal that set up victory (*right*). His advance is arguably the greatest testament to the management skills of Mourinho, indisputably Chelsea's finest ever manager (*opposite*).

'It is the way of our press sometimes that they look for faults in a team. But hopefully we are producing something here that people will look back on and say, "What a great team they had over a length of time." We've only done it two seasons and we want to keep doing it for a good few more.'
Frank Lampard (2006)

'I think Chelsea in these two years have proved that history is to be changed, and because of the second title, we are not a Blackburn that was champion once, isolated, and after that is miles and miles away from it. Chelsea is not any more an isolated situation. It's back to back. And if, in the next five years, we can be a total of three or four times champions, definitely it's an era where Chelsea becomes powerful.'

José Mourinho (2006)

'It was so important to win this game [against Manchester United]. I know we only needed a point but we wanted to show we are the best side this season. To do it at home in the way that we've done it, beating a great side 3-0, is special. It is a magic day all round and even better than last time.'   Joe Cole (2006)

Index

About the Author

Football, history and music writer, and a Matthew Harding Upper season ticket-holder, Rick Glanvill has contributed to Chelsea's official publications since 1993. He has written well over a dozen books, including the highly acclaimed *Rhapsody In Blue* and *Chelsea FC: The Official Biography*, as well as the *Urban Myths* series, featured in the *Guardian*. He is also a broadcaster and regular on 'Chelsea TV' and is the club's official historian.

Rick is a north Londoner, and is forever grateful to his Arsenal-supporting father for allowing his toddler sons to support 'the boys in Blue'. His own two sons, Oliver and Alfie, were given no such choice.

Picture Credits

The publishers would like to thank everyone who helped in researching and providing pictures for this book. Special thanks go to Marcel Adamson, Colin Benson, Andy Cowie, P.J. Crook, Simon Garfield, Paul Joannou, Jackie Law, Liz Parsons, David Ransom, Francis Serjeant, Richard Shepherd and Catherine Theakstone. Thanks also to Carole McDonald for all the special photography.

Action Images/Darren Walsh 219tr; Beefeater Brewery 24; British Library 14, 28–9, 29r, 61r, 132; Bridgeman Art Library 120–1; Martin Burgess 88 (*background*); Chelsea Football Club Museum 15, 17r, 98, 99, 102b, 103l, 126l, 128, 129b, 149tr, 151r; Colorsport 46l, 123, 129 (*background*), 138, 144b, 145, 146, 150, 151l, 159tr, 160, 163bl, 166, 166–7, 172r, 175r, 177tr, 185, 189; Empics 16b, 17l, 60, 81, 87, 90r, 104l, 106r, 112–3, 119t, 119br, 127, 133, 136, 142r, 143, 148, 158l, 161, 163t, 164t, 165m, 165br, 168, 169l, 172l, 174, 175l, 176, 184, 184–5, 188, 189, 192, 194, 195bl, 195br, 196, 199, 202t, 204, 205, 206–7, 208, 209, 210, 211, 214, 215r, 216, 217, 218tl, 218–9, 220, 221; Simon Garfield 180–1; Mike Geen 11t, 13, 16t, 18, 20, 22, 23, 25r, 27b, 28b, 32, 33, 37m, 43l, 45b, 46r, 47, 48, 49, 50, 51, 52–3, 58, 59, 61b, 62, 63, 66, 70–1 (*background*), 74–5, 78, 79, 80, 88m, 88b, 96–7, 102t, 103r, 108t, 109, 134–5, 139r, 141l, 144t; Getty Images 34–5, 41, 44t, 54–5, 56–7, 64–5, 76, 83, 86, 92, 93, 94, 95, 101, 104r, 106l, 117, 119bl, 122, 124, 126r, 129t, 139l, 149b, 158–9, 159br, 163br, 186–7, 215l, 218bl; Paul Goulden 105, 115; Hammersmith and Fulham Archives and Local History Centre 10r, 25l, 82, 152, 153; Hugh Hastings 173tl; George Hilsdon 29b; *Illustrated London News* 21, 26, 27t, 30–1; John Ingledew 170–1, 198; Paul Joannou 36, 77; London Metropolitan Archive 10l, 12, 38–9; Roy Mitchell 88r, 89l, 89r, 91; Offside Sports Photography 167, 177bl, 202b, 203; Ordnance Survey 8–9, 11b; David Ransom 70b, 71b, 72, 73; Ben Radford 182–3; Science & Society Picture Library 137; Richard Shepherd 67, 68, 69; Robert Stein 44m, 45ml, 141r; Albert Sewell 128 (*background*), 164b, 165t; Joe Smith 149tm.